AMERICAN PRISONER OF WAR CAMPS

IN MONTANA AND WYOMING

KATHY KIRKPATRICK

AMERICA
THROUGH TIME®
ADDING COLOR TO AMERICAN HISTORY

For Gary Reeves, for sharing photos of his amazing POW collection

America Through Time is an imprint of Fonthill Media LLC
www.through-time.com
office@through-time.com

Published by Arcadia Publishing by arrangement with Fonthill Media LLC
For all general information, please contact Arcadia Publishing:
Telephone: 843-853-2070
Fax: 843-853-0044
E-mail: sales@arcadiapublishing.com
For customer service and orders:
Toll-Free 1-888-313-2665

www.arcadiapublishing.com

First published 2019

ISBN 978-1-63499-194-0

Typeset in 10pt on 13pt Minion Pro
Printed and bound in England

Contents

List of Illustrations

Introduction

America is a nation of immigrants, so hosting prisoners of war (POWs) from their homelands brought mixed feelings among the civilians and military in the communities where the prisoners were housed and worked. For many farmers who had immigrated to the Midwest, being able to contract for German POW labor not only eased the labor shortage, but it also brought the opportunity to speak their native language, perhaps to learn about family and friends left behind when they moved to America. It also often gave them the opportunity to provide additional food for men who worked hard for them and shared their friendship. Although these Americans had sons fighting in the war, they were more aware of the lack of choices these German prisoners had in their own lives than those who had not left an oppressive homeland.

The same situation applied to Italian immigrants and Italian POWs with the additional benefit of a less strained relationship after Italy became a part of the Allied cause in September 1943. The resulting friendships (and some marriages) show the very positive results of their experiences under very difficult circumstances.

In fact, when German-American or Italian-American families were given permission to hire prisoners of war to work on their farms or canneries, they were being given a measure of approval often missing in their own communities. In 1940, 330,000 Germans and 694,000 Italians had registered as aliens. Those not living on the coasts were not displaced but suffered the name-calling and ostracism promoted by the government and media directed at those groups of people during that time to promote the war effort. They could be arrested just for translating English into German for an aged grandparent.

The stories shared in the course of researching this topic include a moving description by a young Girl Scout raising the flag while a truck load of prisoners passed by, with tears in their eyes. Even as a child, she understood that those men deeply loved and missed their children, who were now living in harm's way.

Following the war, some of these farm families corresponded with the former prisoners until their deaths. A treasure trove of about 350 letters and photos from German former prisoners has recently been discovered in a home in Tennessee. They are now housed at the Lipscomb University in Nashville. They met by working on that farm, then kept in touch over the years. However, it was secret. The letters were found in a cereal box in a closet and even the children of this woman did not know about them.

Left: From "una Storia Segreta" by Lawrence Distasi. The licensing metadata from the picture claims that it is a "work prepared by an officer or employee of the United States Government as part of that person's official duties."

Below: Entrance to the Vatican Secret Archives. (*Author's collection*)

German prisoners of war at Fort Douglas (UT) in 1917 (crews of German ships). (*Utah Historical Society*)

For many years into the 1970s and 1980s, and as late as 2009, there were reunions and family trips made by former prisoners to their old camps and the farms where they worked. They also visited the graves of their comrades who did not survive to go home at the end of the war.

Of the half-million German immigrants arriving in the United states from 1947–1960, several thousand had spent time here as prisoners of war. The same can be said of Italian immigrants after World War II. They had friends and good experiences here that motivated them to move here themselves.

Even among those enemy aliens who were forced to repatriate at the end of World War II in exchange for Americans and for other reasons, the vast majority had agreed to the arrangement because it guaranteed them the ability to return to the U.S. at a later date. They later used that agreement to return home to the United States. That included Germans, Italians, and Japanese.

Prisoners were moved between Service Command Areas in 1943 as the U.S. built more camps and received more prisoners from overseas. Later, the prisoners were moved within a Service Command as necessary to provide seasonal labor on farms and in canneries as well as other work necessary for civilians as well as the military population.

Using a variety of sources in the United States and Italy, the complete story will be told. Sources cited include military records now housed at the National Archives II (in College Park, MD), documents from the Italian Army Archives in Rome (*Stato Maggiore Esercito*) and *L'Ufficio Informazione Vaticano per I prigionieri di guerra istituito da Pio XII* in the Vatican Secret Archives, as well as many books, articles, websites, and photographs.

Also utilized are interviews with former POWs, guards, translators (and their families), and many other sources both published and unpublished. Their experiences will also be compared to those of German POWs and internees held in America during World War I.

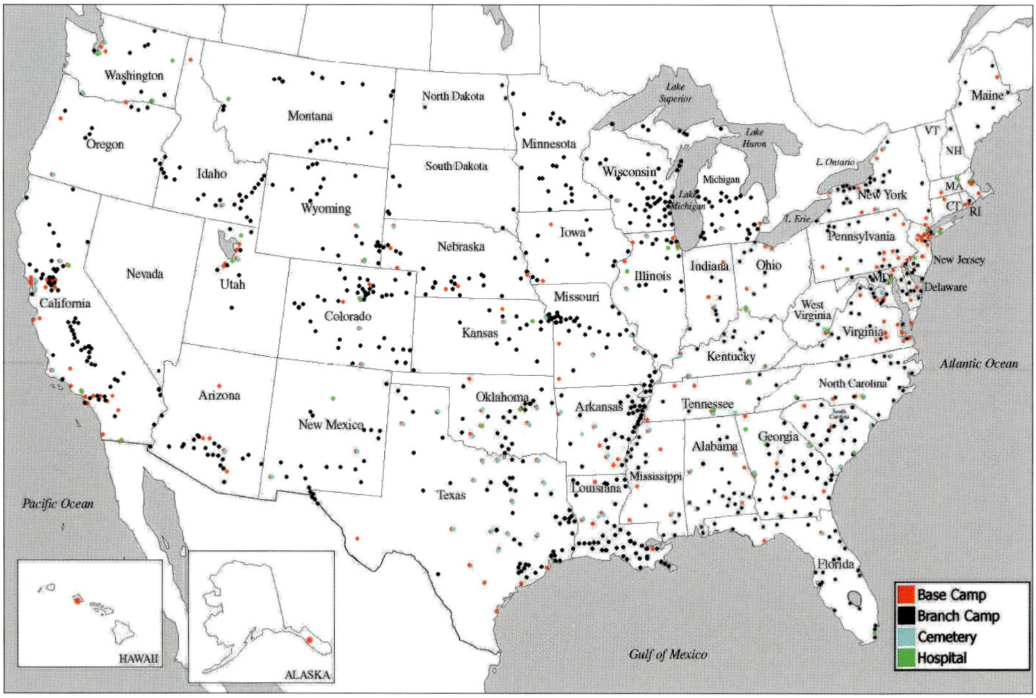

Map of POW Camps and Hospitals Across America. (*John Saffell*)

Background

By the time we entered World War II (WWII), almost the whole world was at war. This situation included large numbers of POWs which could no longer be supported by the limited resources of the British and French who captured many of them, primarily in North Africa in 1939.

The U.S. had already prepared plans for camps to house large numbers of enemy aliens, so assisting with prisoners captured by the British was easily incorporated into those general plans. It was determined early that the U.S. would not be imprisoning as many enemy aliens as first planned. The number of resident aliens who matched the original enemy alien profile was much larger than anticipated, so implementing that original plan was not possible.

During World War I (WWI), only 1,346 POWs were held on United States soil. They were the crews of German military ships lying in U.S. ports when the war began. They were held in the same three locations as civilian enemy aliens, plus six additional branch locations for a total of 5,887 prisoners of war. All other prisoners of that war captured by the U.S. were held in France.

Those U.S. locations included the following:

War Prison Barracks #1—Fort McPherson, East Point, GA—100 prisoners maximum.
War Prison Barracks #2—Fort Oglethorpe, Catloosa County, GA—800 prisoners maximum.
War Prison Barracks #3—Fort Douglas, Salt Lake City, UT—406 POWs and 786 enemy aliens.

On March 21, 1918, the POWs were transferred from Fort Douglas to Fort McPherson. On July 19, 1919, 108 conscientious objectors arrived at Fort Douglas from Fort Leavenworth, KS. They were housed in the compound left vacant by the POWs.

Branch camps under the camps in GA:

Camp Devens, Ayer, MA—100 prisoners maximum
Camp Grant, Rockford, IL—100 prisoners maximum
Camp Jackson, Columbia, SC—100 prisoners maximum
Camp Sevier, Greenville, SC—100 prisoners maximum
Camp Sherman, near Chillicothe, OH—100 prisoners maximum
Camp Wadsworth, Spartanburg, SC—100 prisoners maximum

Left: Monument to German POWs from WWI at Fort Douglas, UT. The U.S. did not separate the enemy aliens from the POWs, so only two of the twenty-one men on this list were POWs. (*Author's collection*)

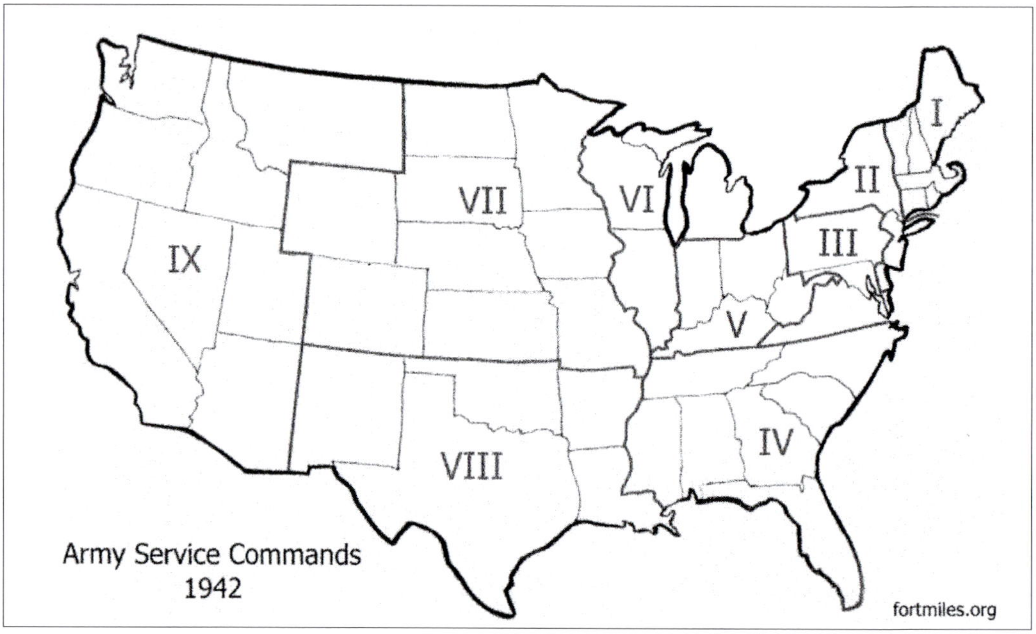

Below: U.S. Service Command areas map. (*National Archives and Records Administration II in College Park, MD, Record Group 389*)

These camps were run by the Provost Marshal General's Office (PMGO) of the U.S. Army. Initially, there were no distinctions between captured German sailors and enemy aliens rounded up from across the U.S. However, it soon became apparent that the two groups were quite different, and efforts were made to put different groups into different camps.

Another camp, called an Internment Camp, was established at Hot Springs, NC and run by the Immigration and Naturalization Service (INS). It held 2,200 Germans from commercial ships in U.S. ports when war broke out in 1914. They were placed at Hot Springs in May 1917 for the remainder of the war. Burials from this location were removed to Chattanooga National Cemetery after that war.

Preparing for War

The military headquarters/training for the 9th Service command moved inland from The Presidio of San Francisco, CA to Fort Douglas, UT at the end of 1941 to make it less vulnerable to a Japanese attack.

The U.S. needed:

1. Labor, since most able-bodied young men were expected in military service and efforts to recruit women into the workforce had only limited success. However, "Rosie the Riveter" became iconic and female pilots as well as clerks (military and civilian), nurses, teachers, and many other occupations gained workers from this effort. Those numbers decreased immediately after the war when the men returned home, but steadily increased as time passed.

2. Supplies for military troops overseas as well as military troops and civilians at home included timber, cotton, tobacco, food (planting, harvesting, canning, fishing), clothing, arms and ammunition and transportation vehicles for land, sea and air.

3. Building and maintenance of new and expanded military installations as well as roads, railways, airfields, dams, and camps for POWs and enemy aliens.

Train at Utah ASF Depot. (*Special Collections Department, Stewart Library, Weber State University*)

Global Situation

POWs held by the British and French were straining their limited supplies so they needed to be farmed out to other Allied nations (Algeria, Australia, Canada, Egypt, Great Britain, India, Kenya, Libya, the Middle East, South Africa, and the U.S.).

POWs were being held in the various theaters of war, but the numbers were much greater than could be used for supply and support behind combat lines. Great Britain held 23,000 German and 250,000 Italian prisoners in August 1942. Plans were made to transport them to places where their care would not remove men from combat and where their labor could be used to ease shortages caused by men away from home.

Generally, ships carrying supplies and men into the European and Mediterranean theaters of war were used to transport POWs back to America, Canada, Australia, etc. While many POWs worried about getting bombed or torpedoed by their own nations, there were few incidents. The SS *Benjamin Contee* was torpedoed off the coast of Algeria on August 16, 1943, by German aircraft. The ship proceeded to Bone, to Algiers, and then to Gibraltar, where emergency repairs were made, then to New York City, arriving January 29, 1944. The bodies of thirty-six unidentifiable Italian prisoners (900 British-held Italian prisoners had been on this ship before the attack) were removed from the most damaged part of the vessel and buried at Long Island National Cemetery.

The German POW population in the U.S. in May 1942 was only thirty-one with one Japanese POW. There were no Italian POWs here at that time.

The Italian POWs were captured by British, French, and American troops between 1939 and 1943 in North Africa and Europe. They first arrived in the U.S. in early 1943 through the New York Port of Embarkation.

For the captured officers and naval crews, interrogation centers were their first stops in America. Fort Hunt, VA, was the first of these centers. These interrogators denied torture and criticized the Bush administration when they were honored near Alexandria as part of the U.S. Army's Freedom Team salute program in 2007. The National Park Service (NPS), particularly the George Washington Memorial Parkway (which now contains the former Fort Hunt), is interviewing veterans of P.O. Box 1142 (as it was known then) to tell their story. The former interrogators include John Gunther Dean, later a career Foreign Service officer and ambassador to Denmark who said "We did it with a certain amount of respect and justice." George Frenkel said, "During the many interrogations, I never laid hands on anyone." He said, "We extracted information in a battle of the wits, I'm proud to say I never compromised my humanity."

Above left: Vincenzo Lo Giudice is shown here with his Italian Army friends in North Africa. *ICourtesy of his daughter, Carmelina)*

Above right: Byron Hot Springs (CA) back door, the entrance for the POWs, Joint U.S. Army and U.S. Navy interrogation center. (*Carol A. Jensen, historian at Byron Hot Springs*)

The second interrogation center was Byron Hot Springs, CA, also known as P.O. Box 651. Following the example of the British to gain maximum cooperation with excellent living conditions, this former resort spa was used primarily for the highest-ranking German officers and Japanese naval crews while Fort Hunt was used primarily for German naval crews. Information gained at Fort Hunt and Byron Hot Springs was also used later in the murder trials of naval POWs accused of murder in the camps.

The third interrogation center appearing on the camp lists as "restricted listing", the same designation as the two locations above, has recently been exposed as Pine Grove Furnace, NY.

These interrogation centers were run by a combination of Military Intelligence, an agency of the Adjutant General's Office (G-2), and the Office of Naval Intelligence (ONI). Since this was against Geneva Convention rules, they were listed on PMGO lists of POW camps as "restricted listing" camps to conceal their locations.

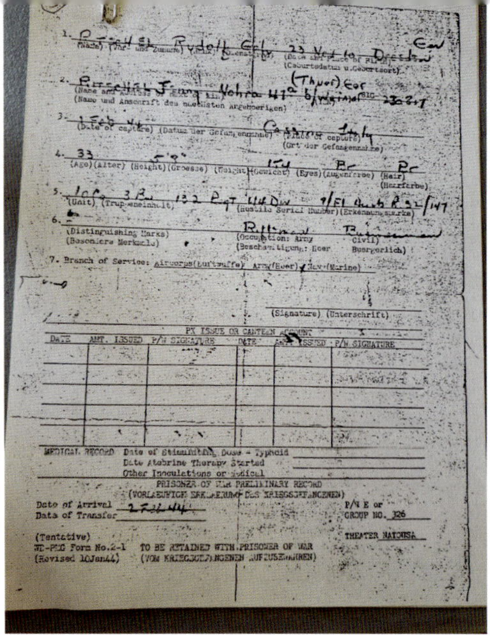

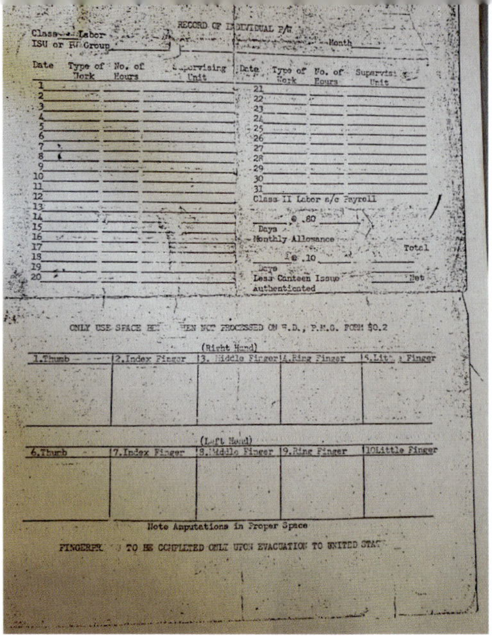

Above: This preliminary record was kept by Rudolf Ritschel and given to Lowell Bangerter, a German professor who translated when the former POW returned to the logging camp where he lived near Dubois. (*Steven Banks*)

Below left: This ID card for Mario Turrini was created at Camp Como, MS. Note that the ID number was crossed out when they realized he already had a POW number assigned by the British, who had originally captured him. In the far-right column, you can see that he had coins from France (from his service in Tunisia), plus coins from Italy (from his Italian Army pay) and Greece (his last duty station before Tunisia). (*Courtesy of his son, Marcello, who lives in Italy*)

Below right: This card for Mario Turrini was created at Camp Ruston, LA, his location after processing at Camp Como. It shows that in May 1944, he was transferred to Camp Hereford, TX. This is part of the sorting process and he was categorized as not cooperative since he did not sign up to be a co-belligerent in the Italian Service Units (ISU) after the fall of Mussolini. In September 1944, he was transferred to the Seattle Port of Entry, particularly Fort Lawton from which he sailed two weeks later for duty at POW Camp APO 950 (a.k.a. Fort Armstrong), Honolulu, HI. The Italian prisoners were not sure where they were going and there were rumors that they would be sent into combat zones in the Pacific theater.

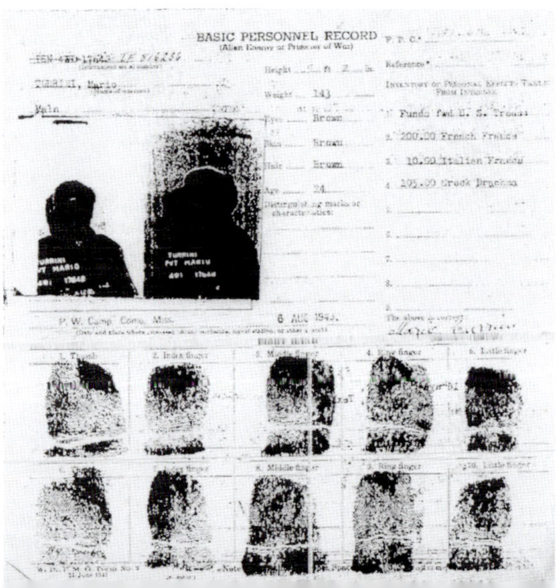

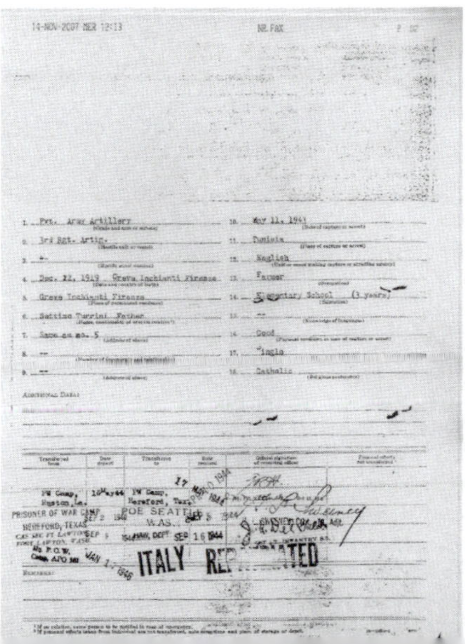

Planning and Building the Camps

Initially, enemy alien camps were planned for 100,000 internees. However, after it was determined that original parameters for designating enemy aliens as potential threats were too broad and could not be implemented because of the vast numbers of people involved, the camps under construction were repurposed as POW camps. They expected to fill them with POWs already captured by the British, about 100,000.

Lessons learned in WWI led to the separation of POWs (under the PMGO of the Army) and enemy aliens (under the INS within the Department of Justice (DOJ)). Also in the wake of WWI were the agreements made at the Geneva Convention in 1929. It was determined that the U.S. would (usually) follow such agreements not only because of the legal obligations, but also in hopes of reciprocal good treatment by our enemies.

Among those soldiers captured in German uniform were men who considered themselves another nationality, such as Austrian, Czech, Swiss, Italian, Russian, Mongol, Hungarian, Romanian, and more. Among those captured in Japanese uniform were Koreans. Among those captured in Italian uniforms were Slavs (present day Croatia, Bosnia, and Slovenia), Albanians, and Ethiopians. It was quickly learned that these groups needed to be separated in the POW camps both at home and abroad. In many of these groups were men who claimed U.S. citizenship. Their trials were postponed repeatedly until the end of the war when they were sent back to the nation in whose army they had been captured.

Only one of the POW camps had previously been used as WWI POW camp, Fort Douglas, UT. Some were already military installations, like Fort Jay, NY. Some were former Civilian Conservation Corps (CCC) camps, like Fort Hunt, VA. Many were new purchases, like Camp Monticello, AR.

There were several potential standard camp plans, adapted to different climates and geographical considerations, but ultimately, each camp was unique in its layout due to geography and transportation infrastructure. In addition to building barracks, mess halls, warehouses, administrative buildings, and a hospital, the first commanding officer of the Utah ASF Depot POW camp, UT, designated 50 acres nearby to grow crops to help feed the POWs. The crop yield was so bountiful it was shared with the Depot cafeteria, the Depot quartermaster, Bushnell General Hospital (in Brigham City), and the Ogden Air Service Command at nearby Hill Field. A similar assortment of buildings and garden areas was described at most other base camp locations.

Camp Douglas, WY, was built in ninety-two days by Peter Kewitt construction company from Omaha, NE. The buildings were wood-framed with asphalt shingle siding, which was considered sufficient for the few years that the war might last.

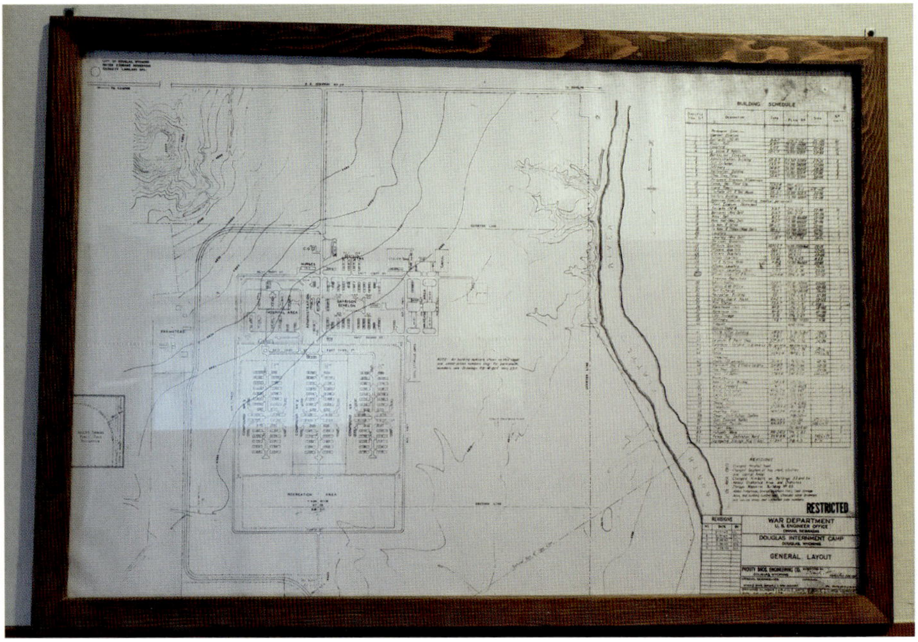

These plans for Camp Douglas show three compounds (using barracks housing fifty men each) to house the prisoners. The cemetery is not labeled, but I suspect it at the far upper right, at the end of the road in an unlabeled area with a boundary marked.

Garden at Utah ASF Depot. (*Special Collections Department, Stewart Library, Weber State University*)

Italian prisoners of war in freight yard at Utah ASF Depot. (*Special Collections Department, Stewart Library, Weber State University*)

The U.S. men who worked at the Camp Douglas Fire Department, with Fay Harris at the front. (*Betty Alberts*)

Above: The POWs who worked at the Camp Douglas Fire Department. (*Betty Alberts*)

Below left: This view of Camp Douglas from the guard tower was located at Wyoming State Archives. (*Department of State Parks and Cultural Resources website*)

Below right: This view of the double fence at Camp Douglas from the guard tower was located at Wyoming State Archives. (*Department of State Parks and Cultural Resources website*)

Managing the Camps

Security was a primary concern. Guards were a combination of military (often older men and wounded combat veterans) and civilian. Sometimes, long-lasting friendships developed between the guards and the POWs they watched, particularly among the interpreters.

In a successful effort to conserve manpower, it was the experience at Utah ASF Depot, UT, that one woman with a dog could patrol the same area as two men.

The POW work details were supervised by guards armed with carbines and rifles. Originally, the ratio was one guard to ten POWs, but over time diminished to one guard to thirty-two prisoners. When U.S. Army personnel was not available, the base commander could supply guards from other sources. Handcuffing or abuse was forbidden. Each of the guard towers in the compound was occupied by a guard equipped with machine guns.

Sometimes, the U.S. Army translators were also guards, like Thomas M. Todaro, who worked at Camp Monticello and later at Fort Leonard Wood, MO. Translators (usually U.S. military) were assigned to camps. However, U.S. military translators for Italian Service Units (ISU) were assigned to the units which moved from camp to camp as needed to provide services.

The POWs were soon discovered to be an uneasy (sometimes dangerous), mix of several nationalities, languages, and ideologies; regardless of their uniform. They were then segregated by nationality and politics and rank. In many camps, the officers were simply held in a separate compound from the enlisted, as directed by the Geneva Convention. However, compounds at Camps Beale, Blanding, McCain and Papago Park were designated for German Naval crews. Camp Alva was for Nazis. Camps Blanding, Campbell, and Devens were anti-Nazi camps. Camps Hereford, Monticello, and Weingarten were for Italian fascists. These divisions into Nazi and anti-Nazi were based on judgments made by G-2, the Army Intelligence unit.

The generalities do not take into account transfers from camp to camp that were frequent and based on additional factors, such as work, health, and relationships. Most POWs did not accurately fall into the above categories; they were young men who grew up in societies with mandatory youth groups and mandatory military service whose families were living in Nazi-controlled locations.

After initial interrogation, the German generals were placed at Camps Clinton and Dermott while Italian generals and officers were at Camp Monticello. Additional German officers were held at Crossville.

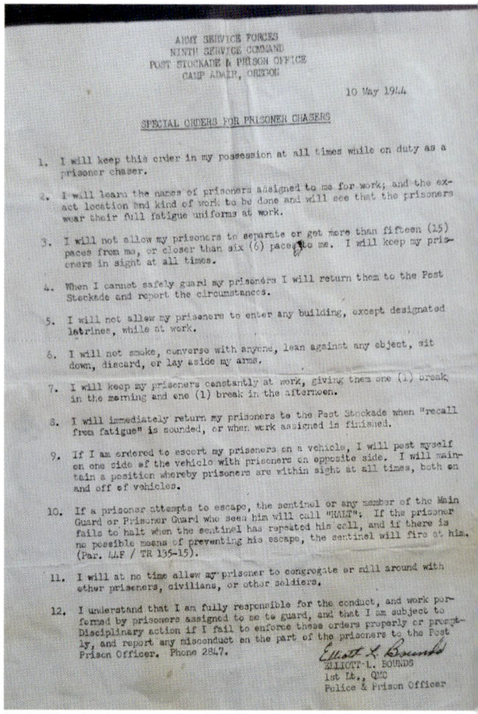

ARMY SERVICE FORCES
NINTH SERVICE COMMAND
POST STOCKADE & PRISON OFFICE
CAMP ADAIR, OREGON

10 May 1944

SPECIAL ORDERS FOR PRISONER CHASERS

1. I will keep this order in my possession at all times while on duty as a prisoner chaser.

2. I will learn the names of prisoners assigned to me for work; and the exact location and kind of work to be done and will see that the prisoners wear their full fatigue uniforms at work.

3. I will not allow my prisoners to separate or get more than fifteen (15) paces from me, or closer than six (6) paces to me. I will keep my prisoners in sight at all times.

4. When I cannot safely guard my prisoners I will return them to the Post Stockade and report the circumstances.

5. I will not allow my prisoners to enter any building, except designated latrines, while at work.

6. I will not smoke, converse with anyone, lean against any object, sit down, discard, or lay aside my arms.

7. I will keep my prisoners constantly at work, giving them one (1) break in the morning and one (1) break in the afternoon.

8. I will immediately return my prisoners to the Post Stockade when "recall from fatigue" is sounded, or when work assigned is finished.

9. If I am ordered to escort my prisoners on a vehicle, I will post myself on one side of the vehicle with prisoners on opposite side. I will maintain a position whereby prisoners are within sight at all times, both on and off of vehicles.

10. If a prisoner attempts to escape, the sentinel or any member of the Main Guard or Prisoner Guard who sees him will call "HALT". If the prisoner fails to halt when the sentinel has repeated his call, and if there is no possible means of preventing his escape, the sentinel will fire at him. (Par. 44F / TR 135-15).

11. I will at no time allow my prisoner to congregate or mill around with other prisoners, civilians, or other soldiers.

12. I understand that I am fully responsible for the conduct, and work performed by prisoners assigned to me to guard, and that I am subject to Disciplinary action if I fail to enforce these orders properly or promptly, and report any misconduct on the part of the prisoners to the Post Prison Officer. Phone 2847.

Elliott L. Bounds
ELLIOTT L. BOUNDS
1st Lt., QMC
Police & Prison Officer

Above left: POW farm labor with guards. (*Gary Reeves' collection of POW artifacts*)

Above right: Instructions for POW guards, issued at Camp Adair (OR). (*Gary Reeves' collection of POW artifacts*)

Below: This British issue dog tag for an Italian-enlisted POW was on display at the March Air Field Museum display on Camp Haan (CA). (*Author's collection*)

Right: Thomas M. Todaro, guard and translator. (*Courtesy of his son, Robert*)

Below: Board at Fort Devons (MA) showing those POWs who could work without a guard. (*Gary Reeves' collection of POW artifacts*)

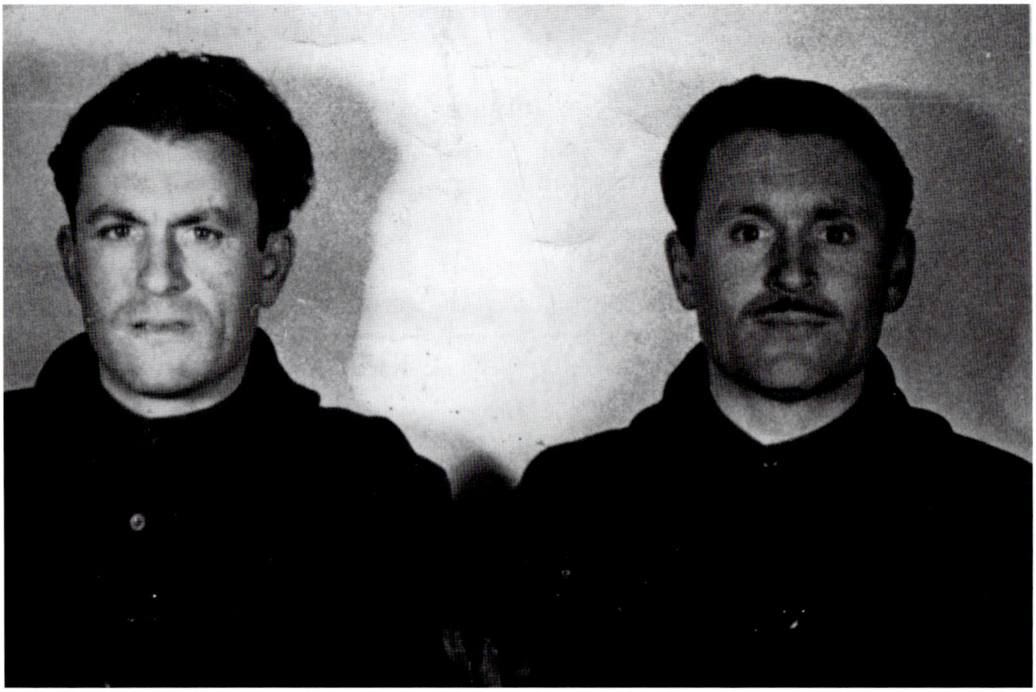

Orazio and Angelo Vecchio, brothers and Italian prisoners at Utah ASF Depot. (*Courtesy of Orazio's grandson, Orazio Vecchio, living in Italy*)

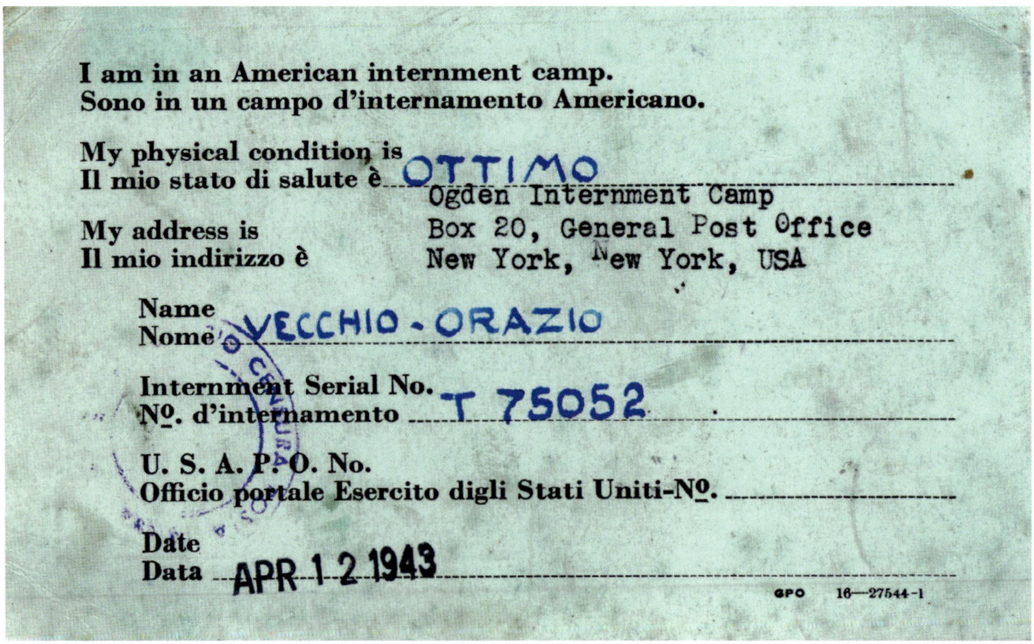

I am in an American internment camp.
Sono in un campo d'internamento Americano.

My physical condition is
Il mio stato di salute è OTTIMO

My address is Ogden Internment Camp
Il mio indirizzo è Box 20, General Post Office
New York, New York, USA

Name
Nome VECCHIO - ORAZIO

Internment Serial No.
N⁰. d'internamento T 75052

U. S. A. P. O. No.
Officio portale Esercito digli Stati Uniti-N⁰.

Date
Data APR 12 1943

GPO 16—27544-1

Standard POW form, filled out for Orazio Vecchio. (*Courtesy of his grandson, Orazio Vecchio*)

Giovanni D'Onofrio (third from left) and POW friends at Utah ASF Depot. (*Courtesy of his children, Vincent, Orazio, and Janice*)

Carlo Selmi and POW friends at Utah ASF Depot. (*Courtesy of his son, Andrea, living in Italy*)

G-2 interviewed these officers, however the highest-ranking officer in these interrogation teams was a Major, so not perceived by the POWs as qualified to deal with an officer of higher rank. Consequently, cursory and sometimes erroneous conclusions were drawn, heavily influenced by other high-ranking enemy officers who were invited to participate.

A glaring example is the input of Italian General Trezzani who used the opportunity to cast doubt (and worse, calling another Italian general a Nazi). He used this ploy on officers of similar rank to promote himself with the Americans. He used it to great advantage to become the head of the Italian Service Units (ISU) in the U.S. and later in charge of rebuilding the Italian Army in post-war Italy.

Additionally, Italian Royalists and career army were considered fascist while German career army were considered Nazi, simply for participating in youth groups (required) or in support of Franco (military service) in Spain. There was so much more to the story.

Public opinion was most loudly expressed by those with the greatest fear of enemy camps in their towns, or by those who hoped to profit from the use of POW labor in their businesses. Most Americans viewed the new camps with caution, but acceptance, and gradually came to appreciate the additional civilian jobs and affordable labor source. Some even developed friendships which lasted long after the war ended.

Each prisoner was processed either when captured or when they arrived in the U.S. This process included searching, delousing, disinfecting, fumigation, bathing, registration, clothing issue, quartering, and medical inspection.

Life in the Camps

The maximum number of German POWs held in the continental U.S. was 371,683 in May 1945. Italian POWs (continental U.S.) reached a maximum of 51,156 in November 1944. Japanese POWs (continental U.S.) reached a maximum of 5,413 in August 1945. There were POW camps in every state except Vermont, plus the territories of Hawaii and Alaska.

The POWs were placed into companies of 250 men each, eight companies to a compound (2,000 men), with two compounds at Ogden ASF Depot in 1943. Later, one compound at Ogden ASF Depot was composed of Italian Service Units while the other housed German POWs who were willing to work there. They were the first camp to work the two groups together, with Germans supervising Italians and the opposite.

Each base camp had a station hospital, staffed by both Americans and POWs. Utah ASF Depot station hospital had 100 beds, like most station hospitals. Since many POWs arrived in poor health due to long imprisonment and poor diet (both before and after imprisonment), that hospital admitted over 2,000 men by June 1944 after opening only eighteen months earlier.

Housing and furnishings at first met, and then exceeded the Geneva Convention requirements. Since the camps were in different locations, some utilized barracks and some hutments (smaller housing units) while the temporary and seasonal camps often used tents. The Geneva Convention required mattresses only for officers. Eventually, most permanent camps had mattresses, pillows, and pillow cases on iron and wooden beds for enlisted men as well as officers.

General hospitals, run by the Surgeon General of Army Service Forces (ASF), were in each region, utilizing a POW wing to facilitate security. In 1944, they became more specialized to receive all patients from theaters of operations, plus patients needing specialized treatment in the zone of interior.

Those station hospitals with airfields were overseen by the Air Surgeon of the Army Air Force (AAF). In 1944, regional hospitals (a new designation), station hospitals, and convalescent centers were now run by both the ASF and AAF. The regional hospitals were to serve as general hospitals for zone of interior patients. These designations are rarely mentioned in the population lists in the National Archives.

The station hospitals were generally staffed with an American officer of the Medical Corps and three POW attendants with medical training. The surgical staff included an American Medical officer, a nurse, an enlisted man, and three POW attendants with medical training.

POWs also served as lab technicians. The hospital mess was under the mess officer with a civilian nurse and a mess sergeant. It was staffed by two U.S. Army mess sergeants, one POW mess sergeant, and four POW cooks. Provisions were made for special diets.

Mental patients in Utah were sent to Bushnell General Hospital, UT, while extreme cases were sent to Mason General Hospital, NY. Dental care was also provided at the station hospitals for the POWs treating abscesses, and doing extractions, fillings, and gum treatments. At Utah ASF Depot, over 17,000 dental cases were treated during the year of 1943–1944.

Upon arrival, the POWs were issued clothing and blankets that were maintained and replaced as needed. The Red Cross in New York was issuing two pairs of blankets per man and a uniform that might be the dark blue with white PW lettering, or an old U.S. Army uniform, plus the uniform he arrived wearing. Not many had overcoats; some came with English overcoats, black with a black diamond on the back.

The POWs were supposed to be adequately, comfortably, and properly clothed in accordance with the climate conditions in which they lived and worked according to the Geneva Convention of 1929. The War Department later determined that dark blue was a preferable uniform color since it would not be mistaken for the American khaki. They were also provided with woolen underwear, cotton underwear, woolen socks and cotton socks, woolen shirts and cotton shirts, two pairs of trousers in either wool or denim, two cotton coats in wool or khaki, a wool overcoat, a raincoat, woolen caps and hats, cotton hats and caps, shoes and overshoes, gloves, and two heavy woolen blankets. When an item wore out, it was immediately replaced. The clothing was class X or class B, American issue.

Some camps had laundry facilities with machines while some had wash rooms where laundry was done by hand.

Education included classes in English, history, and democracy plus clerical and equipment training. Supplies were provided for many art projects and newsletter production.

Newspapers were produced by the prisoners at most of the larger camps. There is a collection of Italian POW newsletters at Utah State University. There is a large collection of German POW newsletters at the Library of Congress. Many of these newsletters can be found at local colleges and historical societies.

Their food was the equivalent of that issued to American servicemen (type A field ration), according to the Geneva Convention, although substitutions were made to recognize ethnic preferences. The Italian POWs had an increase in rice, spaghetti, macaroni, noodles, and pasta with decreases in meats and baked beans. Germans had an increase in potatoes and a decrease in beans. Meals were served three times daily. Special menus were prepared on Thanksgiving, Christmas, New Year's, and other holidays. For many prisoners, these rations exceeded their military experience. The average prisoner at Utah ASF Depot gained 15 pounds.

The POWs were their own cooks and bakers, being paid the same wage as those working in all occupations both in and outside of the camps. However, each camp commander had some autonomy and after the liberation of concentration camps in Germany, some camps restricted food allowances for POWs well below Geneva Convention (Hereford, TX, is infamous for its dietary cuts in 1945).

Many services were available for POWs, some in accord with the Geneva Convention and some additional benefits. They included canteens and camp stores where a POW could spend the pay (in coupons) he earned working on such items as beer, cigarettes, and gold jewelry (high-quality necklaces, wedding rings, and rosaries were in high demand by the Italian POWs at Utah ASF Depot). The profits from the sales were returned to the POWs in the form of free beer, cigarettes, and theater tickets.

Utah ASF Depot hospital grounds. (*Special Collections Department, Stewart Library, Weber State University*)

Utah ASF Depot hospital steps. (*Special Collections Department, Stewart Library, Weber State University*)

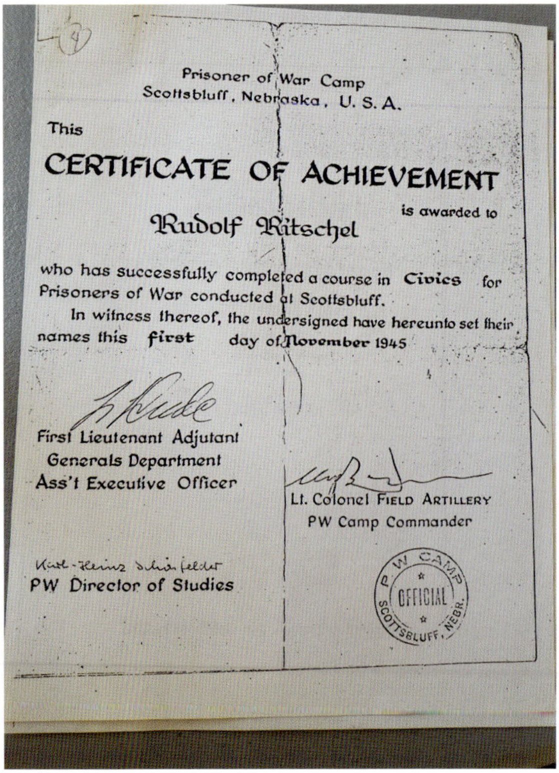

Above: Utah ASF Depot POW class with civilian instructor and U.S. Army guard. (*Special Collections Department, Stewart Library, Weber State University*)

Left: Certificates were given to the POWs who completed a variety of courses in the camps. This achievement in civics was awarded to Rudolf Ritschel and given to Lowell Bangerter, a German professor who translated when the former POW returned to the logging camp where he lived near Dubois. (*Steven Banks*)

POW newspaper from Fort McClellan, AL. (*Gary Reeves' collection of POW artifacts*)

Some beautiful art was created in the camps; this piece from Colorado shows a sense of humor as well. (*Gary Reeves' collection of POW artifacts*)

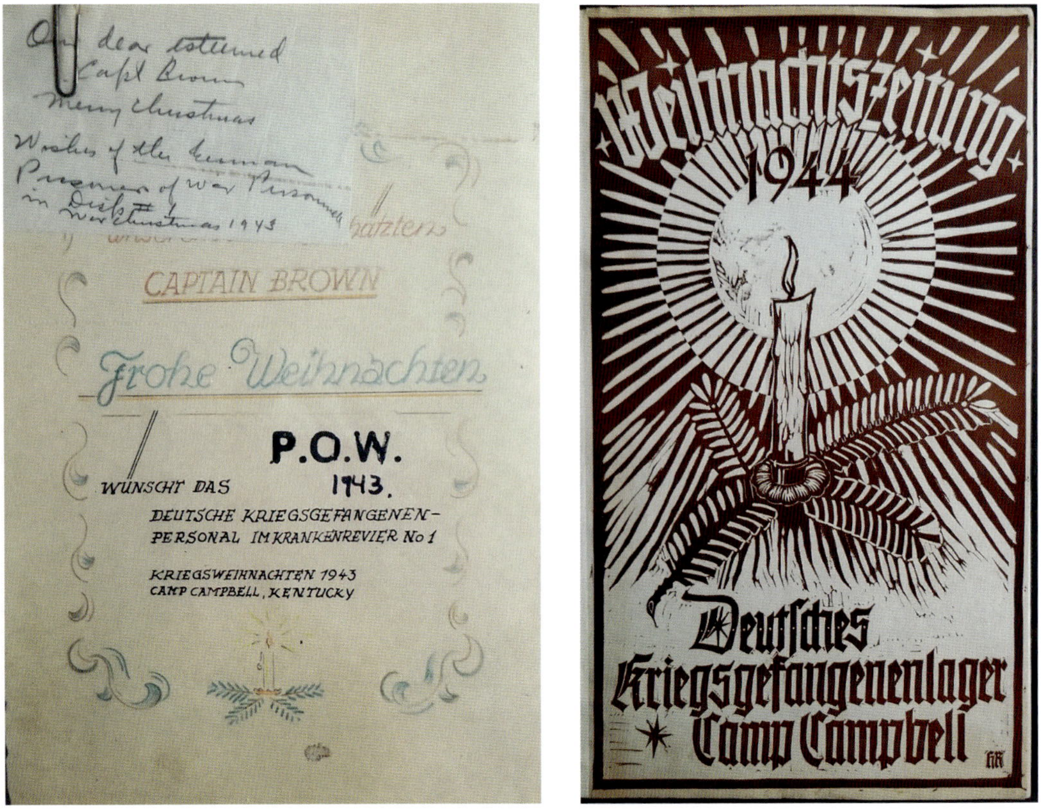

Christmas card from a German POW at Camp Campbell (KY). (*Gary Reeves' collection of POW artifacts*)

Some POW photos show the decorations (pin-ups) in their personal areas. These could include small pictures of national leaders and flags and emblems, but large displays were limited to funerals and religious services.

Recreation supplies were provided for many sports, although soccer was most popular. Other equipment included baseball, softball, basketball, football, boxing, volleyball, croquet, horse shoes, badminton, and table tennis. Many game sets were also provided for the POWs including dominoes, Chinese checkers, checkers, backgammon, India, bingo, chess, playing cards, etc. The POW often constructed their own volleyball courts, baseball diamonds, and soccer fields.

POW contacts with families and others included inspection visits from the Red Cross, YMCA, Swiss government, and other welfare organizations. Each POW was permitted two letters and one post card per week, written in ink (not pencil). Also, when necessary, one business letter per week was allowed. Special stationary was provided, so it was limited to the lines on the forms. Free mailing was applied to all letters, postcards, and parcels less than four pounds, addressed to or sent by a POW through the U.S. Postal Service. Each POW was also allowed, at his own expense, one prepaid cable or telegram per month. In the event of a serious emergency (death or serious illness), and at the discretion of the base commander, more than one per month may be sent.

Italian POW cooks at Utah ASF Depot. (*Special Collections Department, Stewart Library, Weber State University*)

Utah ASF Depot, Italian POW bakery. (*Special Collections Department, Stewart Library, Weber State University*)

Incoming mail for Italian POWs from relatives in the U.S. was enormous. In two or three months alone, 300–500 packages were received at Utah ASF Depot. The POWs sent many gifts to their relatives in this country and to those outside the continental U.S. Correspondence to POWs was permitted from anyone. However, POWs could only write to and receive packages from family members such as wives, grandparents, parents, siblings, aunts, uncles, children, nieces, and nephews.

Most camps had bands and/or orchestras made up of their POW population. At many locations, concerts were held once a week. The orchestras also played for stage shows and gave monthly concerts. Many instruments were provided by the Catholic church; others were loaned by the Depot Quartermaster. At some camps, the local schools and communities provided instruments.

The ISU band at Utah ASF Depot played for dances each week, both at the POW camp and at St. Joseph's Catholic Church in Ogden. The dances were a good place to meet the local girls. The POWs were taken to the church by bus from the camp. Separate dances (different nights) for officers and enlisted POWs to adhere to Geneva Convention.

Religion was also a part of camp life. At first, religious services at Ogden, UT, were held in the open with an improvised pulpit. Later, a recreation hall was used part time for morning Mass. An empty barrack was utilized as a regular chapel for weekdays. Later, the old Compound One Headquarters building became the Main Chapel and accommodated about 300 POWs for daily Mass. When Compound Two was activated, one of its recreational halls was provided for chapel functions and accommodated about 700. This camp was Italian, so only Catholic services were required. The hospital also held Mass on Sunday. When the camp opened a German compound, a Lutheran minister provided services on Sunday in addition to the Catholic services for the German POWs. Every U.S. camp had a similar regard for religious services.

Ration coupons were issued by each camp, but the format was standardized as shown here of coupons from Camp Livingston (LA), Camp Grant (IL), and Camp Rupert (ID). (*Gary Reeves collection of POW artifacts*)

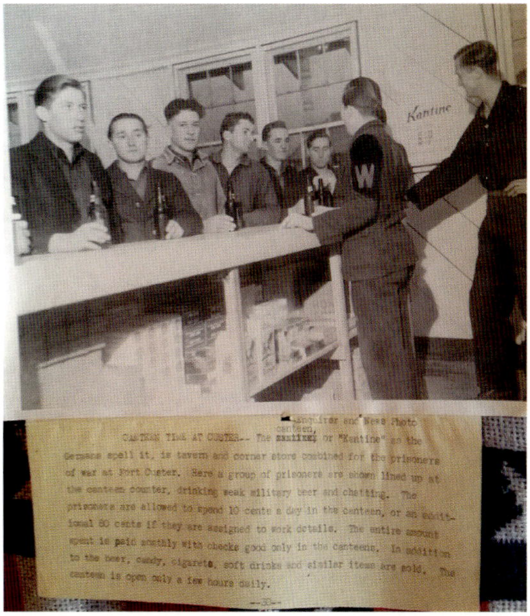

Right: This photo was taken for a news service of the canteen at Camp Custer (MI). (*Gary Reeves' collection of POW artifacts*)

Below: This photo shows the distribution of cigarettes to POWs at one of the camps. (*Gary Reeves' collection of POW artifacts*)

Left: Matchbooks were made for Fort Robinson (NE) and many other camps. (*Gary Reeves' collection of POW artifacts*)

Below: Some camps issued cards for special items, like this beer card. (*Gary Reeves' collection of POW artifacts*)

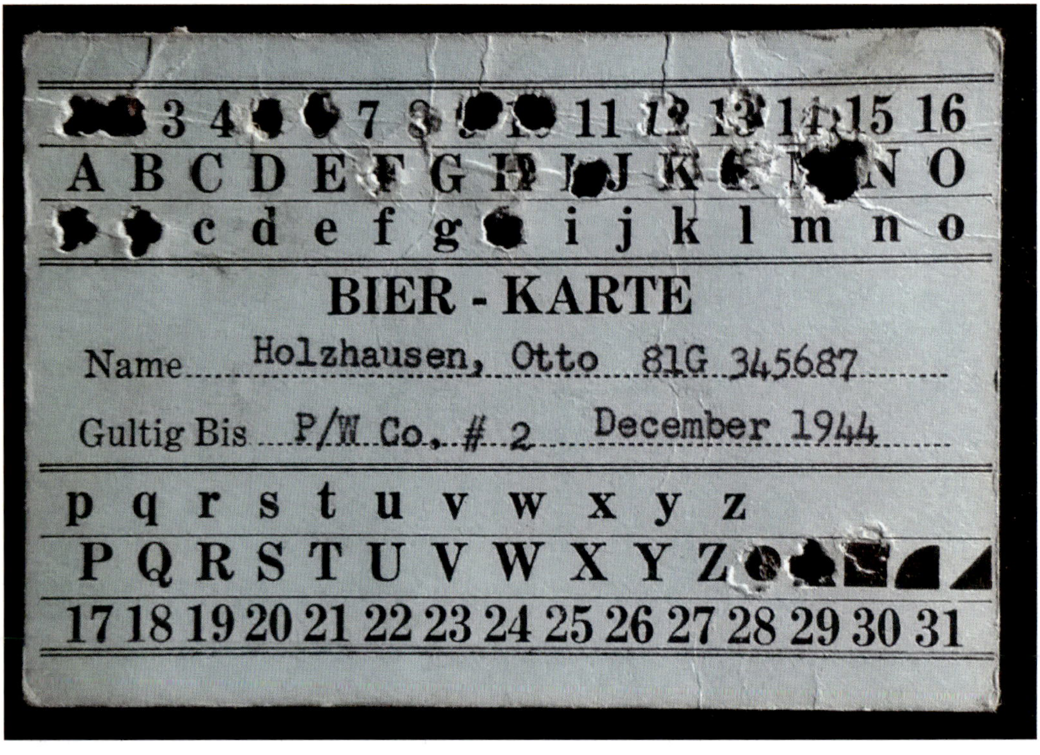

Jewelry box made for Fay Harris by German prisoner

Underside of drawer on jewelry box

Above and below: This jewelry box was made by Adolf Dietz, a German POW held at Camp Douglas, for Fay Harris, one of the firemen at the camp. (*Betty Alberts*)

Underside of lid on jewelry box

Above: Of course, people create art out of whatever is available, as evidenced by this water canteen with inscriptions from this German soldier's time in Africa in 1943. (*Gary Reeves' collection of POW artifacts*)

Below: Barracks at Camp Atterbury (IN). (*Alessandro de Gaetano*)

Above left: Theatrical productions at Fort Lewis. (*Gary Reeves' collection of POW artifacts*)

Above right: POW soccer team at Edgewood Arsenal (MD). (*Gary Reeves' collection of POW artifacts*)

Below left: This letter was sent from a British POW camp in Garian (Libya) to a POW in Camp Wheeler, GA. (*Gary Reeves' collection of POW artifacts*)

Below right: This letter was sent through the Red Cross from a POW Camp in Custer (MI) to a young woman in Austria. Some letters were also sent through the Vatican as an alternative to the U.S. mail. (*Gary Reeves' collection of POW artifacts*)

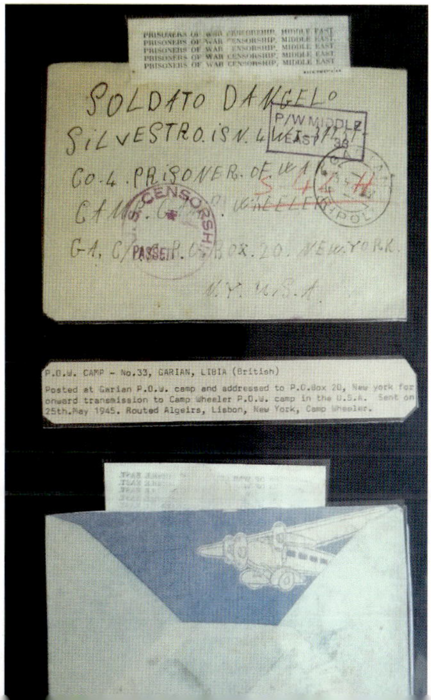

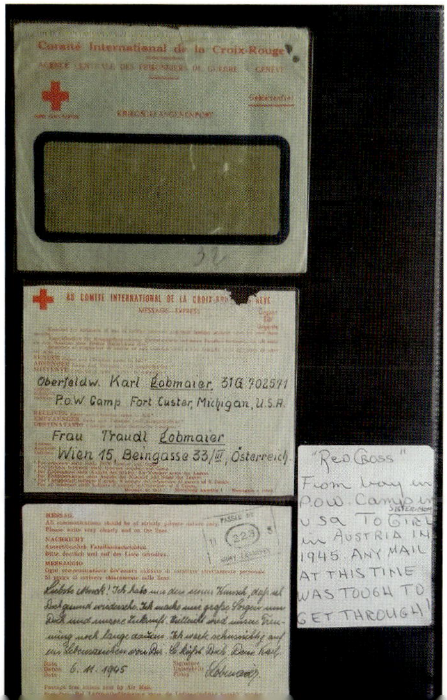

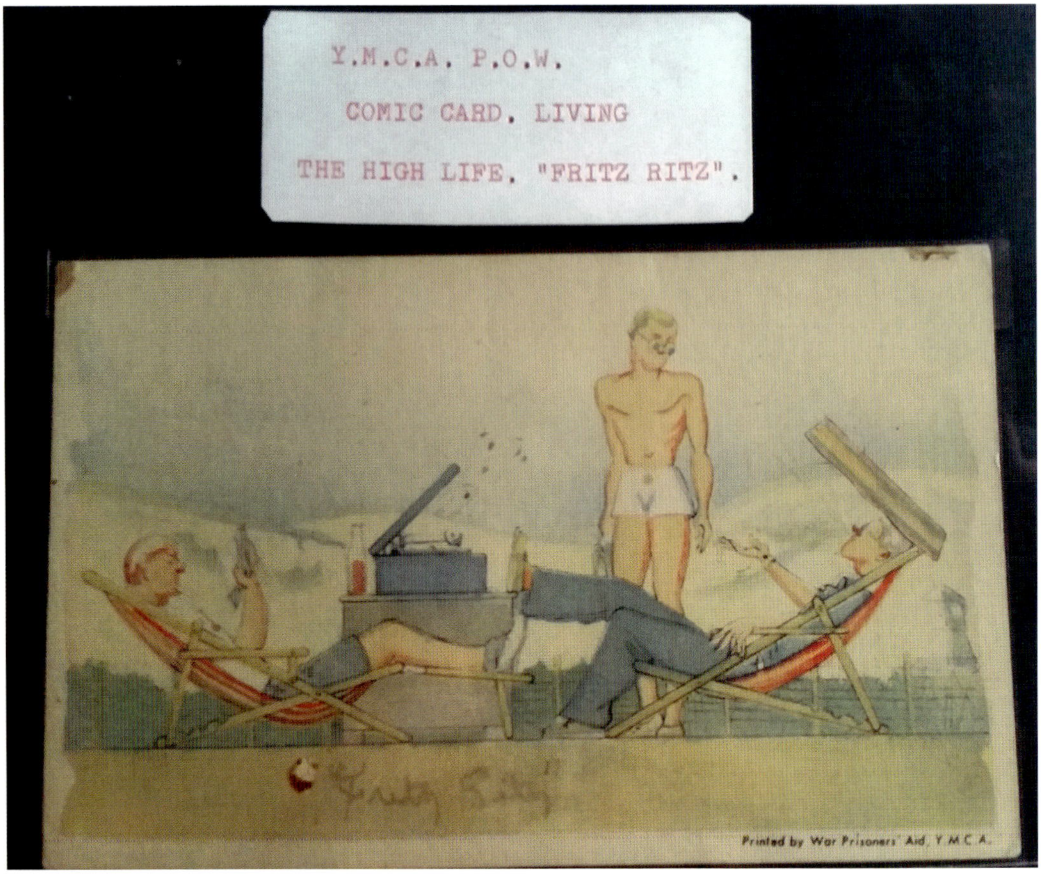

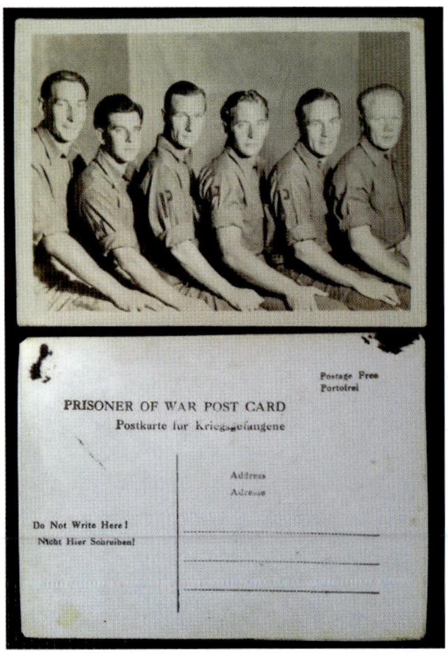

Above: This postcard was designed by a German POW and printed by the YMCA. (*Gary Reeves' collection of POW artifacts*)

Left: Postcard with a group photo of German POWs. (*Gary Reeves' collection of POW artifacts*)

Above: Many camps and military installations had their own postcards. (*Courtesy of Robert Todaro from his father's duty assignment there as a POW translator and guard*)

Right: Postcards with a group photo of German POWs from Camp Swift (TX). (*Gary Reeves' collection of POW artifacts*)

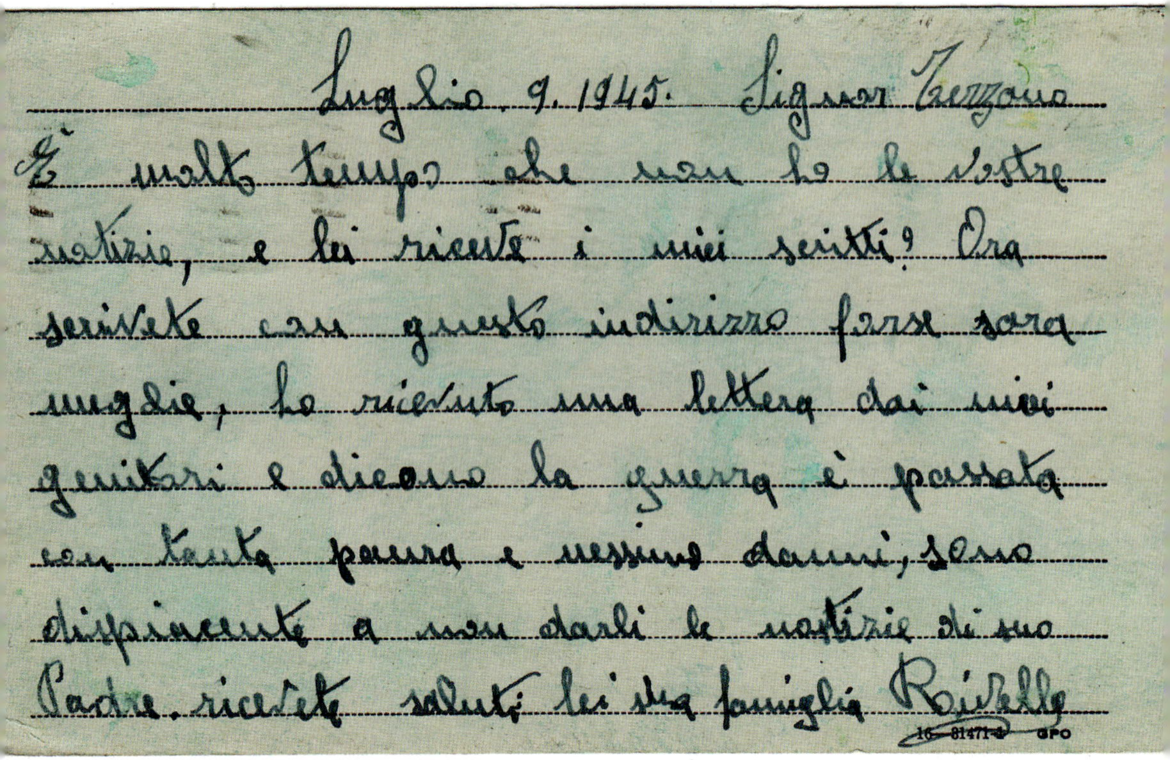
Luglio 9. 1945. Signor Terzano

È molto tempo che non ho le vostre notizie, e lei ricevete i miei scritti? Ora scrivete con questo indirizzo forse sarà meglio, ho ricevuto una lettera dai miei genitori e dicono la guerra è passata con tanta paura e nessuno danni, sono dispiacente a non darli le notizie di suo Padre. ricevete saluti lei sua famiglia Rivella

16—81471-1 GPO

Above and below: POW postcard from Fort Douglas (UT). (*Dennis H. Pack*)

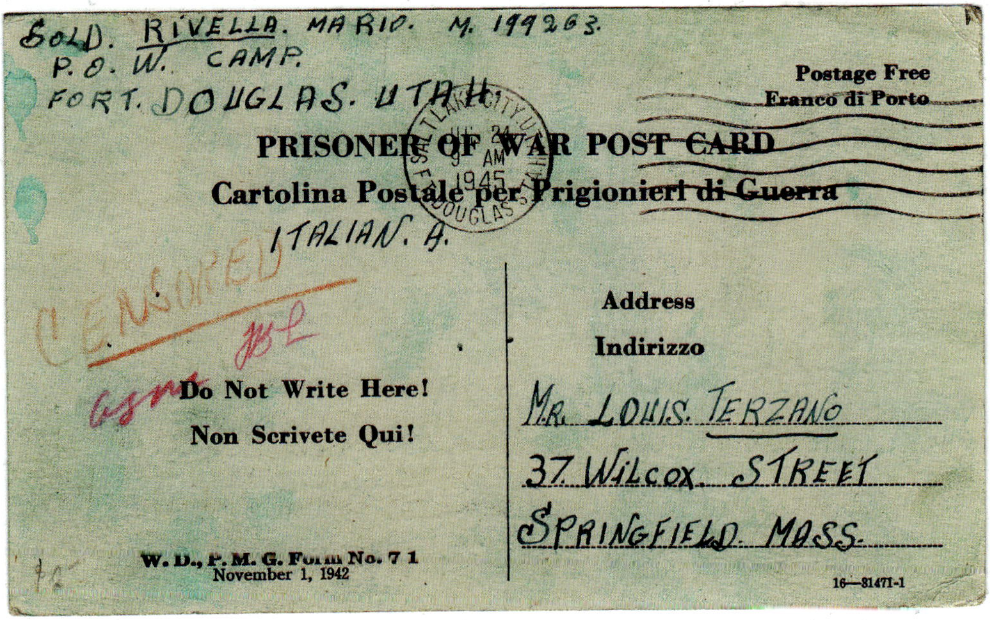
SOLD. RIVELLA. MARIO. M. 199263.
P.O.W. CAMP.
FORT. DOUGLAS. UTAH.

Postage Free
Franco di Porto

SALT LAKE CITY, UTAH
JUL 24 9 AM 1945
FORT DOUGLAS STA.

PRISONER OF WAR POST CARD
Cartolina Postale per Prigionieri di Guerra
ITALIAN. A.

CENSORED

Do Not Write Here!
Non Scrivete Qui!

W. D., P. M. G. Form No. 71
November 1, 1942

Address
Indirizzo
MR. LOUIS. TERZANO
37 WILCOX. STREET
SPRINGFIELD. MASS.

16—81471-1

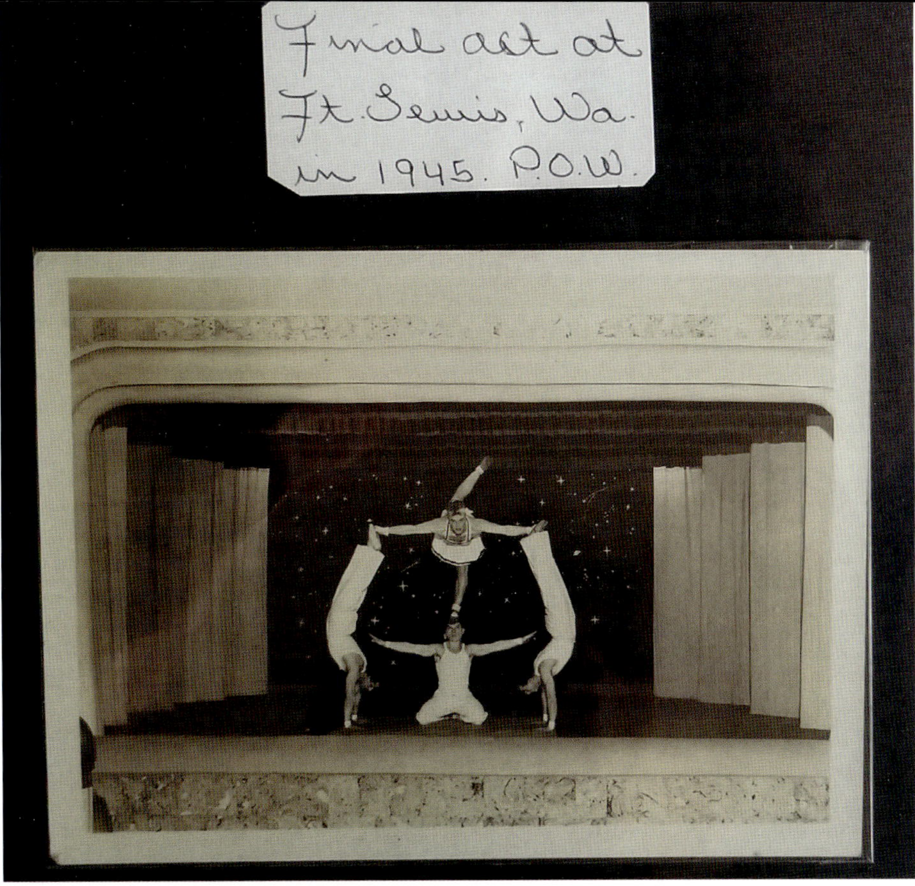

Above: Acrobats on stage at Fort Lewis (WA). (*Gary Reeves' collection of POW artifacts*)

Below: ISU band at Utah USF Depot. (*Courtesy of Andrea Selmi, son of Carlo Selmi, clarinet player in this band (third from left), living in Italy*)

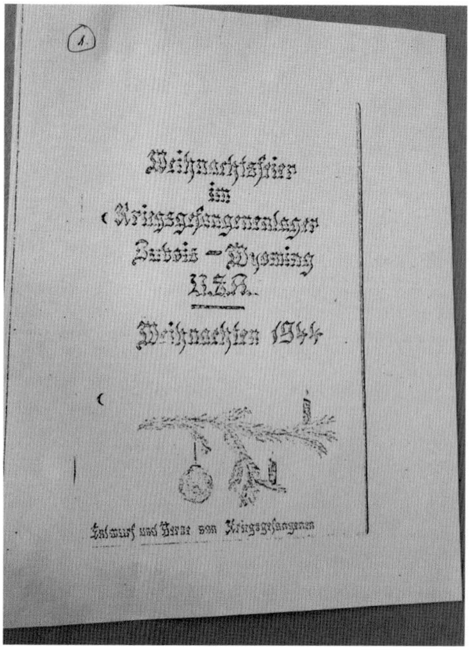

Christmas program at Camp Dubois by and for German POWs. (*Steven Banks*)

While POWs were not allowed to donate blood (prohibited by the PMGO and Geneva Convention), they were allowed to make voluntary contributions to specific organizations, such as the Red Cross and the YMCA. A minor political group at Utah ASF Depot, the Republicans, collected $80 for war bonds and offered to donate blood; they offered the money to the Infantile Paralysis Fund because they believed it was a good cause.

Escapes were expected and did occur at several locations. Most of them were short in duration and distance, usually ending with an easy capture or surrender since the object was just to get outside the fence for a while. Some were more serious, with bigger plans and groups of men, also usually ending in surrender. Just a few men were able to remain at large until many years after the war ended. No reports of sabotage or terrorism were ever associated with these escapes.

Camp Douglas, Wyoming, was the location for three escape attempts. Two POWs were found hiding in a haystack downriver from the camp, both clothed in six pairs of G.I. winter underwear. Three POWs used paper dummies to hide their escape during roll call. Six men escaped from this location, but they were found 25 miles south when they asked which state they were in.

There were pets among the POWs, sometimes traveling with them from camp to camp. POW work included occupations required for the maintenance of the camps, such as cooking, cleaning, clothing and shoe repairs, landscaping, etc.
They also were hired out for canning and farming in the community, including pruning orchards and planting as well as harvesting. They also worked on dams, railroads, orchards, mining, quarrying, and forestry. The businesses and farmers paid the government a minimum wage and the POWs were paid 80 cents a day, comparable to the wage for a civilian day laborer.

Even the Ogden Chamber of Commerce hired POWs, and Italian POWs at Fort Monmouth, NJ, were making violins.

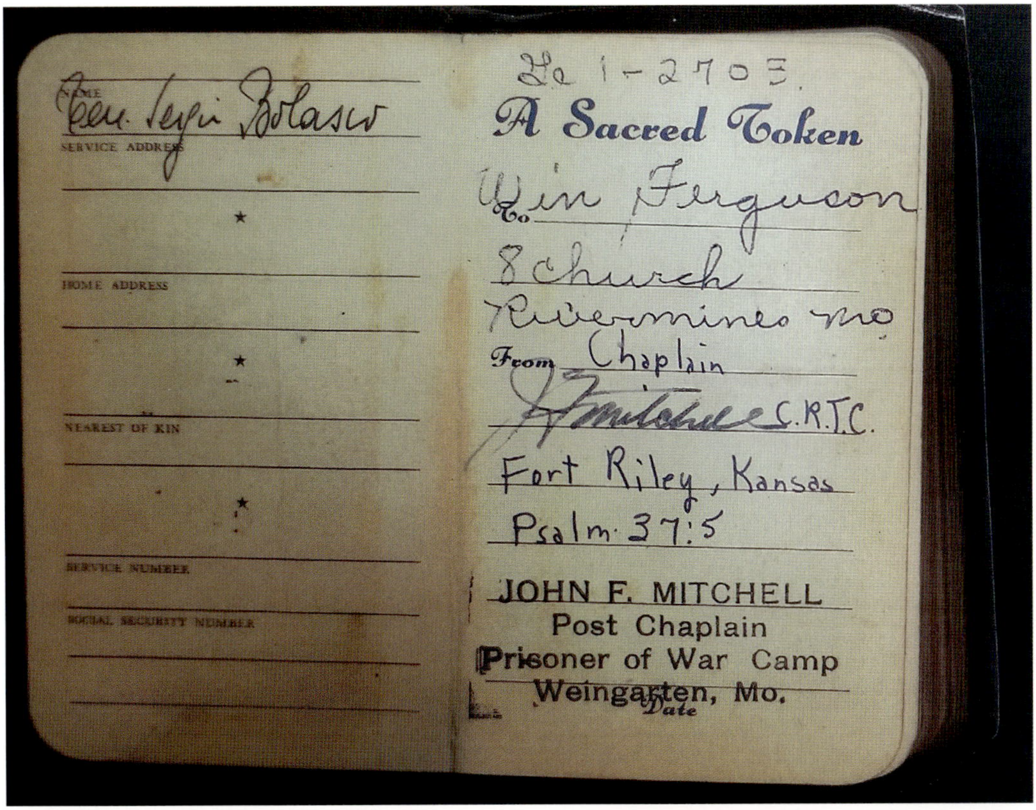

Above: This Bible seems to have gone from Win Ferguson to Italian Lt. Sergei Bolasco after being presented by a U.S. Army chaplain who served at both Fort Riley (KS) and POW Camp Weingarten (MO). (*Gary Reeves' collection of POW artifacts*)

Right: Madonna made and placed at Camp Lockett (CA) near their housing area by Italian POWs. (*Mountain Empire Historical Society*)

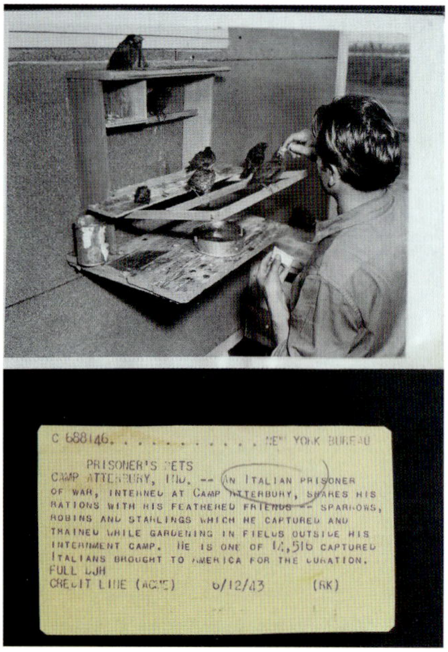

Left: This photo of a POW with pet birds outside the barracks was taken at Atterbury, IN. (*Gary Reeves' collection of POW artifacts*)

Below: A group of Italian POWs at Camp Lockett, CA pose with their priest and their dog. (*Courtesy of Mountain Empire Historical Society*)

Have you seen these five men? They're German prisoners of war who escaped from POW camps—and are still at large in the United States

Curt Richard Westphal

Now 31, Westphal, an ex-sailor and truck driver, broke out of a camp in Bastrop, La., in August, 1945. He is stocky, ruddy and blue-eyed

Werner Paul Lueck

Lueck, now 33, is blond, blue-eyed, of medium height. He weighed 167 when he escaped from Las Cruces, N.M., in November, 1945

Harry Girth

Tallest of the five, Harry Girth is a husky, blond six-footer, born in Poland. Now 27, he broke loose from Fort Dix, N.J., in June, 1946

Georg Gaertner

A former draftsman, Gaertner is 32, tall and fair, with a scar on his left index finger. He escaped from Deming, N.M., in September, 1945

Kurt Rossmeisl

Oldest of group, Rossmeisl is 46, college-educated, speaks English with British accent. Broke out of Camp Butner, N.C., August, 1945

"IT'S EASY TO BLUFF AMERICANS!"

By UNTEROFFIZIER REINHOLD PABEL with BILL FAY

Doubt it? Then read this astonishing adventure story by a captured German soldier who broke out of an Illinois prisoner-of-war camp almost eight years ago, married an American woman, started a small, successful business in Chicago, and might still be at large, if—

As Phillip Brick, he was a respectable family man and rare-book dealer in Chicago, Ill.

In 1953, *Collier's* magazine published a story about five German POW still missing. One escaped from near Bastrop (LA), one from Las Cruces (NM), one from Fort Dix (NJ), one from Deming (NM), and one from Camp Butner (NC). (*Gary Reeves' collection of POW artifacts*)

Other POWs were working on occupations labeled military, such as at hospitals, supply offices, post exchanges, construction, dying uniforms, landscaping, and woodworking.

Sometimes POWs worked on community service projects outside the camp. The Catholic Church of St. Mary's in Umbarger, TX, was beautifully decorated with murals and other artwork by Italian POWs from nearby Camp Hereford.

The POWs were paid a minimum wage consistent with civilian day laborers if they did work (about $30/month for enlisted) or $24 a month for officers who were not allowed to work. Those men who did work were paid $0.80–1.20 each day depending on if working for local farmers or private companies. This was paid to them in coupons they could use at the Canteen, although ISU members could receive one-third of their pay in cash to use in town. ISU members also received pay that was slightly higher (sometimes $1.50/day) to match the pay of American soldiers. That rate of pay was based on their rank in the ISU, not their Italian Army rank. An office of the Italian Army that made sure all the former POWs received their due pay was opened at the end of the war and continued until very recently. I worked in their offices in 2004 and was able to obtain records of transfers from camp to camp and the health record for a POW (with authorization from his son).

Geneva Convention required that officers be separated from enlisted men. They were sometimes in a compound next to the enlisted men and had otherwise the same types of facilities.

Left: Driving railroad ties down the Wind River (tie drive) with labor of German POWs from Camp Dubois. (*The Dubois Museum*)

Below: Murals painted by Italian POWs at St. Mary's Catholic Church at Umbarger (TX). (*Courtesy of John Saffell*)

Above: Clearly, this is not the first time the folks in town have seen POWs going past; the boy on a bicycle is not even looking at them and the teenage girls are interested spectators. (*Gary Reeves' collection of POW artifacts*)

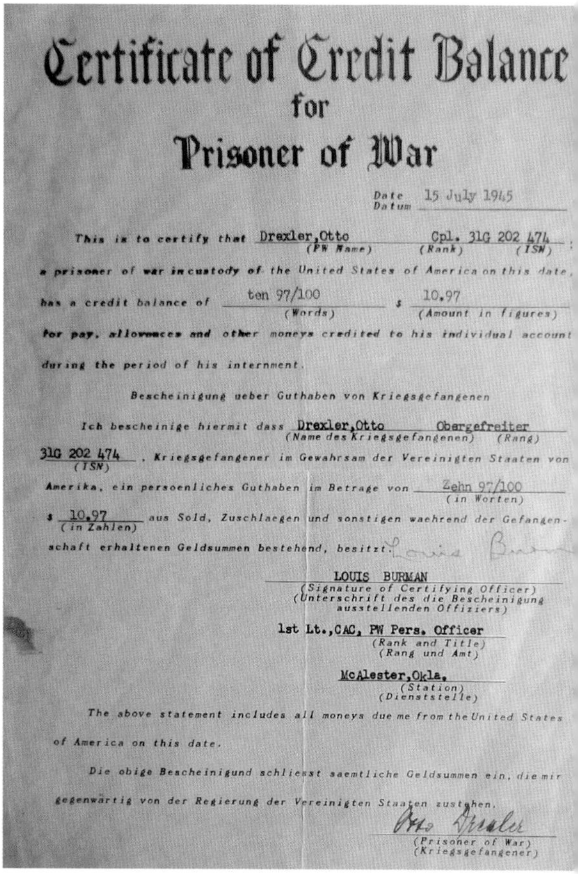

Certificate of Credit Balance for Prisoner of War

Date / Datum 15 July 1945

This is to certify that Drexler,Otto (PW Name) Cpl. (Rank) 31G 202 474 (ISN) a prisoner of war in custody of the United States of America on this date, has a credit balance of ten 97/100 (Words) $ 10.97 (Amount in figures) for pay, allowances and other moneys credited to his individual account during the period of his internment.

Bescheinigung ueber Guthaben von Kriegsgefangenen

Ich bescheinige hiermit dass Drexler,Otto (Name des Kriegsgefangenen) Obergefreiter (Rang) 31G 202 474 (ISN), Kriegsgefangener im Gewahrsam der Vereinigten Staaten von Amerika, ein persoenliches Guthaben im Betrage von Zehn 97/100 (in Worten) $ 10.97 (in Zahlen) aus Sold, Zuschlaegen und sonstigen waehrend der Gefangenschaft erhaltenen Geldsummen bestehend, besitzt.

LOUIS BURMAN
(Signature of Certifying Officer)
(Unterschrift des die Bescheinigung ausstellenden Offiziers)

1st Lt.,CAC, PW Pers. Officer
(Rank and Title)
(Rang und Amt)

McAlester,Okla.
(Station)
(Dienststelle)

The above statement includes all moneys due me from the United States of America on this date.

Die obige Bescheinigund schliesst saemtliche Geldsummen ein, die mir gegenwärtig von der Regierung der Vereinigten Staaten zustehen.

(Prisoner of War)
(Kriegsgefangener)

Right: This form from Camp McAlester (OK) shows the accounting made by the U.S. Army when the POWs were processed to return home. (*Gary Reeves' collection of POW artifacts*)

A Papal Delegate visited the Italian POWs at Camp Weingarten (MO). (*Gary Reeves' collection of POW artifacts*)

Italian Service Units

The fall of Mussolini and resultant change in that government's position in the war from Axis to Allied required some changes regarding Italian POWs. It was quickly determined that releasing them would not be the best solution. The original idea of Italian POWs being organized into units to provide labor similar to the Civilian Conservation Corps (CCC) was first proposed by the U.S. Secretary of War in October 1943. This would require separation of fascist Italian POWs from those willing to work for the war effort as co-belligerents.

> [They would be] attached to and placed under the command of the U.S. Army … Therefore, the plan included these features: (1) Italian prisoners would be organized into numbered Italian service companies consisting of 5 officers and 177 enlisted men … (4) An Italian service unit headquarters would be established under ASF and would be commanded by an American officer … The new plan provided for Italian Service Units (ISUs) to be organized from volunteer Italian PW officers, non-commissioned officers, and enlisted men under approved tables of organization and equipment, less weapons. Initially, two U.S. Army officers and 10 enlisted men were to be attached to each unit for supervision; but these were to be reduced, consistent with efficiency and security, to a minimum of one officer and five enlisted men.

The ranking Italian general over the new ISU on January 26, 1944, Claudio Trezzani, stated:

> The units should be commanded by Italian officers, in this proportion; one first or second lieutenant for 30 to 35 enlisted men (platoon), one captain for 4 platoons (company), one senior officer for 3 companies (battalion), one colonel for 3 battalions (regiment).

That letter is followed in the Italian Army file at Stato Maggiore Esercito in Rome by an apparent American response with no name or date attached:

> It is contemplated organizing Italian Service Units according to American tables of organization with Italian military personnel in all authorized positions, American officers and enlisted men in the smallest possible numbers will be attached as custodians, for liaison, to issue operational directives, sign payrolls and charges, and have general responsibility for the units to higher American authority.

Italian Service Units at Utah ASF Depot. (*Special Collections Department, Stewart Library, Weber State University*)

Italian Service Unit English Class at Camp Warren (WY). (*Gary Reeves' collection of POW artifacts*)

Italian Generals Frattini and De Simone were moved to ISU headquarters at Fort Wadsworth from Camp Monticello.

The ISU program was under the command of Brig. General J. M. Eager, from the PMGO. The ASF retained the responsibilities of plans, policies and procedures as well as the designation and strength of units and training programs and doctrines. Each unit had American personnel of one officer and five enlisted men at a minimum. Service commands were responsible for all other ISU functions and activities. Interviews with former translators assigned to those units confirmed that one American NCO was a translator for the unit.

The ISU had increased responsibilities resulting in increased privileges for the 65 percent of Italian POWs who signed up to serve in Italian Service Units. The new units were activated progressively with 600 POWs organized in the first week of March 1944, 1,000 for the first two weeks of April, 3,000 the third week in April, and 4,000 each succeeding week until completed. While a letter was sent to the camps from Badoglio in Rome, it was vague and general; also, the Italian king never spoke (wrote) on the subject. This left many men in confusion as to the best course of action. Their families were in German occupied Italy and many feared repercussions for such a visible support of their former enemy. The screening from ISU to POW and reverse was continuous to ensure that only the most cooperative POWs were allowed the privileges of the ISU.

Those men who signed the agreement to join the ISU were given new positions and units and now lived in separate compounds than the POWs who did not sign the agreement.

Those POWs who did not join the ISU were classified as Fascist. Instruction in English stressed in these new units, while the same housing and wages applied, with the addition of 10 cents a day for a gratuitous allowance, sometimes more depending on the work and on their ranks in the new units. Two-thirds of the wage was paid in coupons and one-third in cash. Rules against fraternization between members of ISU and American military did not apply. ISU service clubs were created to give them greater access to reading materials and a quiet place to relax since they did not have access to the U.S. Army clubs. Dances and other special events were organized through the ISU service clubs.

Training programs for ISU were the same as for American personnel on similar jobs, less tactics and weapons training.

Work restrictions imposed by Geneva Convention were lifted with the consent of the Badoglio government of Italy, except for combat, work at ports of embarkation within continental U.S., and work with explosives. Their efforts released U.S. personnel for overseas duties and helped to bring about the successful conclusion of the war.

ISU units began to ship to European theater to assist with support and supply from Africa and into Italy as part of the Liberation of Italy in the following theaters of operation: North Africa, Eastern European, and Mediterranean. Apparently, some of these units were moved overseas at the discretion of the ISU command and the PMGO did not always include those units in their reports.

Mail restrictions were reduced to the same standards as American personnel for domestic correspondence. Regulations were the same as POWs for international mail. The new ISU uniforms were the same khaki as U.S. uniforms, with a patch (Italy) on the left shoulder. At least one man was court-martialed for removing the Italian patch on a night out on the town, leading to accusations of being AWOL. However, he was simply reprimanded instead of sent to a POW camp.

The POWs and their employers and guards were not supposed to fraternize. Yet, of course, they did. While some of the initial contact was antagonistic, many friendships and romances

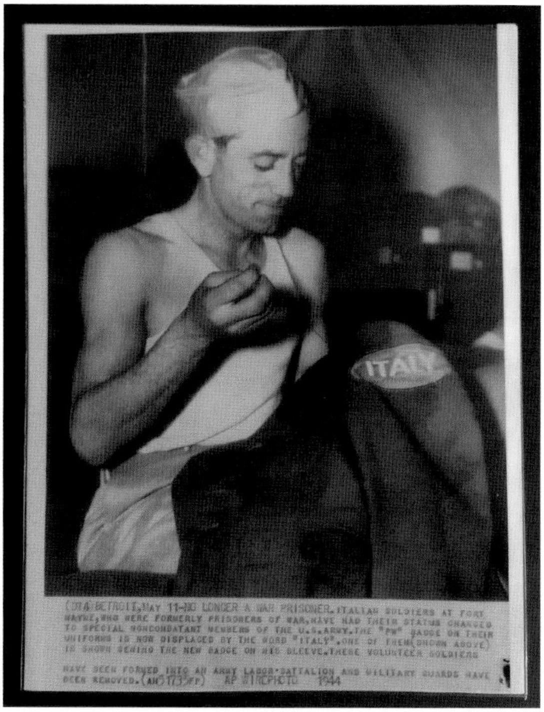

Above left: Sewing on his new ISU patch at Fort Wayne (MI). (*Gary Reeves' collection of POW artifacts*)

Above right: Official photos were taken of the men in their new uniforms. Note that this photo of Vincenzo Lo Giudice, provided by his daughter, Carmelina, does not yet have patches for rank attached.

Below: Italian Service Club at Utah ASF Depot. (*Special Collections Department, Stewart Library, Weber State University*)

resulted. The ISU members did not have those restrictions, often enabling closer relationships.

ISU men were permitted weekend passes when signed out by a sponsor. Many Italian communities utilized these privileges to give some of the ISU men a family gathering, social activity, or dance. Some of the dances at the ISU Service Club included invitations to young women in the community.

Additionally, ISU members were given day passes into town for movies, dances, and just sightseeing. In Ogden, buses were used to transport ISU men from their barracks to St. Joseph's Catholic church in downtown Ogden for dances. Of course, the greatest attraction was meeting and dancing with American girls.

Some of these meetings resulted in marriages. The POWs could not marry, but once engaged, and returned (by June 1946), the troop transports bringing GIs home were taking these women with their escorts to Italy with the proper paperwork to marry so they could return to the U.S. with their new husbands. Several of these couples settled in the locations where they had been imprisoned, met sweethearts, and had friends. Two Italian brothers who had been POWs at Camp Douglas settled in the area. Cesare Obiano married the daughter of the man who sponsored his return to the U.S. A couple of German POWs were sponsored by a local ranch owner, and later bought and ran ranches of their own in the area. That sponsor, Alzira Cross, was a female rancher whose photo standing with her rifle over a dead wolf is more impressive than the fan collection she donated to the Wyoming Pioneer Museum in Douglas.

Some of these meetings had unhappy endings. The local culture was against marrying a man of a different ethnic or religious background, plus some families feared that their girls would follow the men to Italy and never return. So those romances were discouraged, even after they created children. Some of those children were adopted out, while some stayed with their mothers who married other men here in the U.S. after the war. Some of those children are sought their Italian families all their lives. Fortunately, we have assisted with some happy reunions.

Public opinion varied as shown in a variety of newspapers from those years. There were some escapes, usually associated with meeting a girl outside the camp for reasons that had nothing to do with national security.

The Italian POWs held a unique position as both POWs and Allies that created different experiences for them than for their German counterparts. In Montana, Wyoming, and other ISU locations, these differences meant more opportunities to not only work with the residents, but also to socialize with them. The resulting friendships (and some marriages) show the very positive results of their experiences under very difficult circumstances.

Death in the Camps

A total of 1,074 burials—including 880 Germans (includes three Russians, four Austrians, one Yugoslavian, one Czech and one Turk), 172 Italians, twenty-three Japanese (includes one Korean)—out of 1,076 POWs who died while held in the U.S. during World War II.

Many of the larger camps had their own cemeteries. After the war, the cemeteries from those camps, which had been closed and some other locations, were moved to national cemeteries to provide the perpetual care demanded by the Geneva Convention.

While most of the headstones were standard issue for U.S. military, there are some exceptions. At Fort Douglas, Eilert's stone was put up by the POWs with the permission of the camp commander and paid for by the POWs.

The funeral services were often attended by Americans as well as POWs, sometimes also a POW choir and/or band and a symbolic series of shots were fired by a military guard.

Rumors insist that most of the POWs who died here were shipped home. The truth is that the U.S. Government was willing to ship them, if the family bore the cost. Of course, most of the families were simply unable to bear that burden at the end of a war they lost. Only one Italian, Renato Facchini, was returned to Italy before February 1947, while Francesco Erriquez was returned to Italy in 2011. Apparently, none of the Germans were returned since the names in the original reports match the current cemetery records.

Some of the deaths were accidents in the course of work or recreation. Others were later deemed murders by Nazi extremists. Some were suicides, particularly at the end of the war.

There was unrest among the African-American units at Fort Lawton because they were segregated from the other U.S. soldiers, but the Italian POWs were allowed to shop in the Post Exchange with those from non-African-American units. So when one of the Italian POWs was found strangled by hanging, three African-American soldiers were convicted of murder and another forty convicted of rioting. While none were executed, all received discharges for bad conduct which negatively affected the rest of their lives. They were finally exonerated in 2007, primarily because of the excellent research proving their innocence in *On American Soil* by Jack Hamann in 2005. Hamann also raises a suspicion that Olivotto was murdered by a U.S. Army guard who was court-martialed for not being at his post during the time of the death.

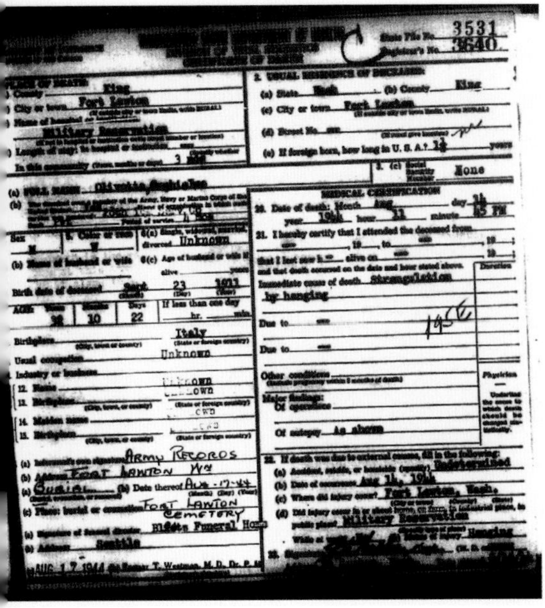

3531
3640
Fort Lawton
Military Reservation
Unknown
Italy
Unknown
Strangulation
by hanging
As above
ARMY RECORDS
FORT LAWTON WN
BURIAL
AUG-17-44
FORT LAWTON CEMETERY
Seattle

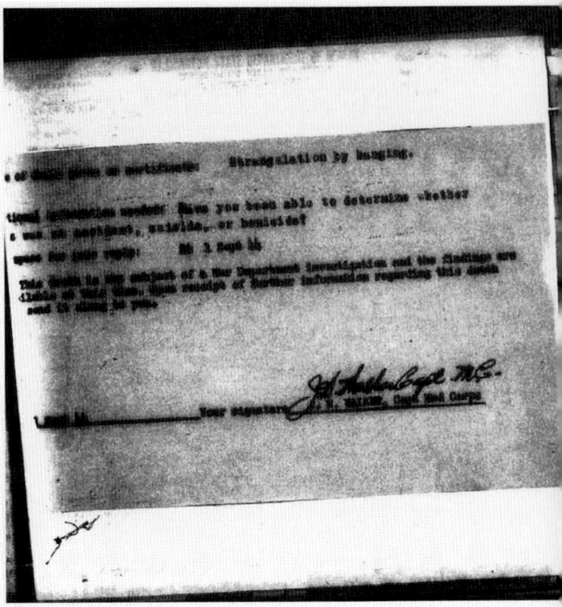

Strangulation by hanging.
Have you been able to determine whether
was an accident, suicide, or homicide?

Above: Note that the cause of death for Guglielmo Olivotto shows strangulation by hanging, but whether murder or suicide is undetermined. (*Death Certificates from Washington State Archives*)

Below: This funeral was held at Camp Monticello, AR. (*Robert Todaro*)

Above: The military honor guard with rifles for a military salute at a funeral at Camp Swift (TX). (*Gary Reeves' collection of POW artifacts*)

Right. Death cards were printed by the family back home in Germany and Italy. This one is for a man who died at Glendon (MN), a temporary camp under Camp Algona (IA). Someone thoughtfully attached a photo of his headstone located at Fort Riley (KS). (*Gary Reeves' collection of POW artifacts*)

Returning Home (1945–46)

The end of the war was cause for celebration for the POWs who could now look forward to returning home. Their newsletters often contained cartoons expressing these feelings.

Certain camps were designated as separation centers (like Haan, CA) and the POWs were moved through them, then on to ports of embarkation on both coasts for the trip home. The first returned were the Italian officers as co-belligerents. The next group was the ISU members, then the rest.

The Geneva Convention of 1929 required that POWs be returned home at the end of a war. However, the large numbers provided some logistics problems. Generally, troop ships bringing U.S. troops home turned around full of POWs. However, treaties with all countries provided that some of the POWs (not ISU) were returned to France, the USSR and Great Britain to assist with reconstruction efforts. Some of the men in Great Britain and France worked there as long as four years before returning home. The USSR finally released the surviving prisoners ten years later.

Warnings were made regarding German POWs scheduled to be returned to their families and homes in the USSR. It was only after the first group was killed on the dock by the crew of the Soviet vessel which met them that other arrangements were made for those men.

Some POWs claimed status as U.S. citizens and requested permission to stay but were returned to avoid the legal complications.

Some locations requested that their POWs stay long enough to complete the fall harvest and that was permitted when it could be arranged. The last POWs were repatriated (out of the U.S.) by June 30, 1946, except 141 Germans, twenty Italians, and one Japanese serving sentences in U.S. penal institutions. Two Germans were not repatriated; they revealed themselves many years later, perhaps more since none are shown as missing on PMGO reports.

A large number of ports were utilized as departure points for the returning POWs. They included: Los Angeles, CA; Charleston, SC; New Orleans, LA; Hampton Roads, VA; New York, NY; Boston, MA; San Francisco, CA; Seattle, WA; and Halifax, Nova Scotia.

Those same troop vessels were used to transport American fiancées of POWs to Naples and Genoa. These American war brides often spent a few months in Italy to complete the red tape required for a marriage there and assisting their new families in rebuilding. They then brought their husbands home to America. These stories were shared by Pat and Maria Pisani and by Beth Giordana, war brides and American girls who made the trip to Italy to marry their former POW husbands.

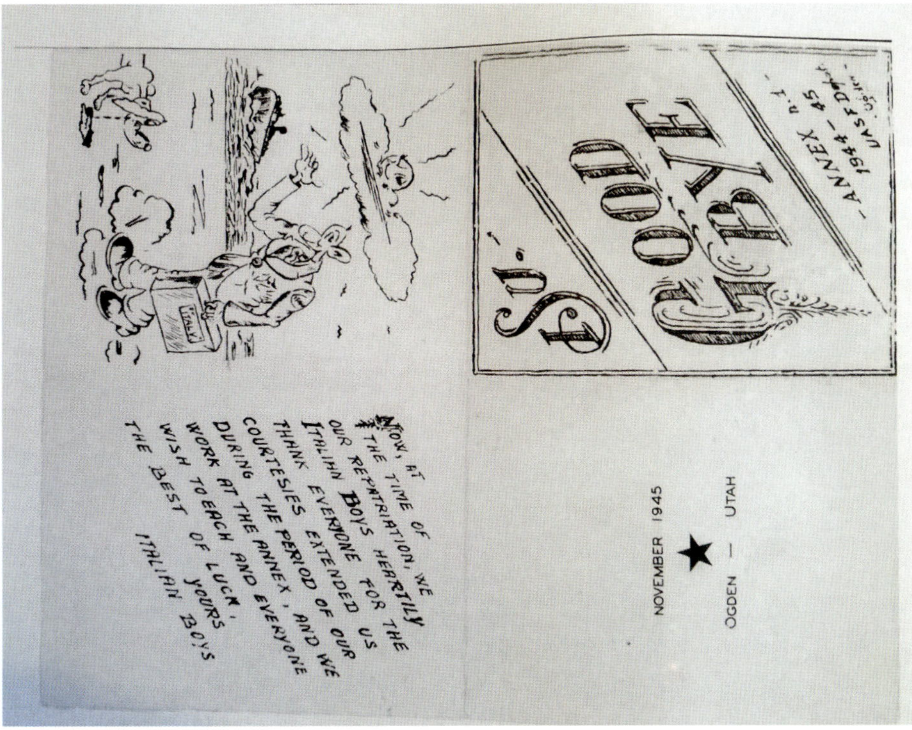

This goodbye note from the Italian boys at Utah ASF Depot was saved by Mario Saggese, one of those boys, and used here courtesy of his daughter, living in the United States.

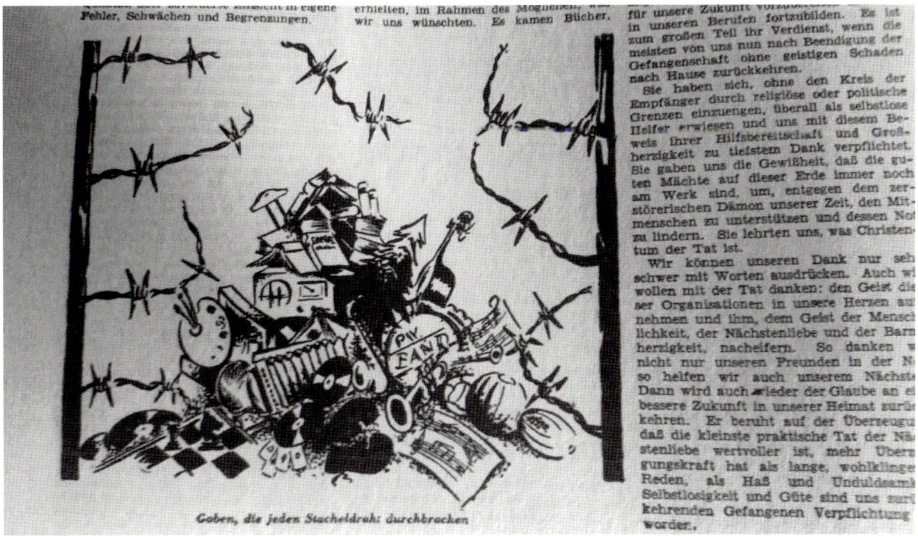

The broken barbed wire and discarded items of entertainment show that while their time as prisoners is ended, so is their leisure time since they now need to rebuild their homes and families. (*Gary Reeves' collection of POW artifacts*)

This cartoon showing the camp for sale is much more lighthearted. (*Gary Reeves' collection of POW artifacts*)

Part of the logistics meant that after the U.S. troops returned home, their European war brides and families were shipped home on the same troop ships, slightly modified to accommodate families with small children. Be sure to see the Cary Grant movie, *I Was a Male War Bride*, which is more funny than factual, but it is based on the real transport of war brides from Europe to America.

Other former POWs made the move to live in the U.S. from ten to twenty years later. They settled in areas where they had worked as POWs, apparently in nearly every location in the country. Only local newspapers have these stories, so it is hard to get statistics. I recently found an article, "Returning to America: German Prisoners of War and the American Experience" by Barbara Schmitter Heisler; the details are in the bibliography.

The trip to marry in Italy was made by a young woman from Louisville, KY, who had met her husband when he was a prisoner at Camp Atterbury, Indiana. They had met at a dance sponsored by the local Italian-American community for the Italian POWs. I met this lovely woman at a POW reunion at Camp Atterbury in 2010 along with her children. They were regular attendees at this annual event and had wonderful stories to share. They also have a display at the Camp Atterbury Museum, across the road from the main gate to Camp Atterbury, now a Reserve Military Training Facility.

TIMELY EVENTS

The News of the World in Pictures

Volume Ten, No. 68, January 19, 1946

LEAVING U. S. FOR SUNNY ITALY

Acme Photo

Timely Events, Inc.

OAKLAND, CALIF.—950 Italian prisoners of war finish first lap of their trip home after leaving POW camp at Warner, Utah, by train. They are embarking at Oakland and will sail through the Panama Canal to New York where the ship will pick up another group. 3,326 Italian POW's, the first group to arrive in Naples.

Fight on!

1946 JANUARY 1946

JOIN THE MARCH OF DIMES

THE NATIONAL FOUNDATION FOR INFANTILE PARALYSIS

Help Fight Infantile Paralysis

Eliminate the scourge of childhood by Contributing Generously

TIMELY EVENTS, published Daily except Sundays and Holidays by TIMELY EVENTS, INC., 236 N. Clark St., Chicago 1, Ill.-By Subscription Only, $78.00 per year. Entered as Second Class Matter, October 26, 1936, at the Post Office at Chicago, Illinois, under the act of March 3, 1879

Above left: These POWs are returning home to Italy in January 1946 from Camp Warner, Utah (Tooele), via Oakland, CA. (*Gary Reeves collection of POW artifacts*)

Above right: These two women have traveled from San Francisco, CA, to New York to board a U.S. military vessel to meet their former POW fiancés in Italy. (*Gary Reeves collection of POW artifacts*)

Left: Of course, most of the former POWs returned to their wives and sweethearts in Italy. This is the wedding announcement for Vincenzo Lo Giudice, provided by his daughter, Carmelina.

Below: This book of art was apparently created during his POW years and published later. (*Gary Reeves' collection of POW artifacts*)

After the War

Some of the camps were determined to be surplus, so the property was auctioned off and the land was sold or transferred to another Federal or State agency. This was a thorough process, leaving behind very little in the way of buildings to mark the former camps today.

Some of the locations had their designations changed from Camp to Fort, some were originally Forts, but called Camps along with the rest in the PMGO records.

The POW personnel records were returned to other nations in whose military they served in 1955.

The German records are now available at:

Deutsche Dienstelle (WASt)
Postfach 51 06 57
D-13400 Berlin
Germany

The Italian records are now available at:

Ministero della Difesa
via Mattia Battistini, 113, 7 Piano
00167 Roma
Italy

The Japanese records are now available at:

Military History Department National Institute for Defense Studies
2-2-1 Nakameguro, Meguro-ku
Tokyo, 153-8648
Japan

The former POWs held in the U.S. mostly held good memories of their time here. Some returned to become U.S. citizens, like Ernst Bulkat who lived in Orem, UT. Information on them can usually be found in local papers in the 1970s and 1980s, when local news groups interviewed them in a resurgence of interest in the history of the area during WWII.

Some former POWs returned as tourists to show their families where they'd spent part of the war. Some groups held reunions of groups of POWs who had been at a particular location to facilitate their return there with some ceremony and lots of memories.

Some diaries and recollections have been published by former POWs. See Erichsen, Heino R. *The Reluctant Warrior: Former German POW Finds Peace in Texas* for the story of a man who later became a U.S. citizen. The grandson of one of the Italian generals, Maurizio Parri, published his grandfather's war time diaries in *Il Giuramento; Generale a El Alamein, prigioniero in America (1942–1945).*

Some former POWs have been gracious about allowing interviews at reunions, such as Adriano Angerilli, Enzio Luciolli, Giuseppe Margotilli, and Fernando Togni (pictured above). Some of the former, guards, prisoners, and their families have become available for interviews using email, like Ernst Bulkat, Mario Iannantuoni, and August Orsini. On other occasions, I am able to interview the children or grandchildren of a former POW in Italy or the U.S.

In 2009, one of the last reunions of former POWs visited the chapel built by POWs at Camp Hereford, TX. This is indicative of a growing awareness that these memories and relationships must be preserved through reunions, books, lectures, and movies.

Some local magazines and newspapers have done stories on the camps and published interviews with former POWs returning to visit, or who had moved back to the area where they had been imprisoned. Some of these have been preserved by the newspaper, some by local historians, colleges, and historical societies.

A documentary video, *Prisoners in Paradise*, DVD, directed by Camilla Calamandrei tells some of the stories of several former Italian POWs.

Some local TV stations did interviews with surviving former POWs living in their communities in the 1970s and 1980s, like KUED and KSL in Salt Lake City, UT. Some local colleges (Special Collections, Stewart Library, Weber State University) created video archives containing interviews of former POWs and their families and former guards and other employees who had interaction with POWs.

Some former POWs, guards, and their families donated their diaries and photos to local historical societies, like Drew County Historical Museum in Monticello, Arkansas. Some donated to the National Archives (NARA) in College Park, Maryland. Some donated to the Stato Maggiore Esercito in Rome, Italy. I expect more will be found in local colleges and libraries in America, Italy, and Germany.

Former guards, like Thomas Todaro and Peter A. Pulia, Sr., also shared their memories in interviews and photos. Some, like Ralph Storm, wrote books about their experiences with POWs.

Even today, I receive email from the children and grandchildren of former POWs to learn more about the experiences of being a POW in the U.S. and the hope of locating records regarding their work, health, and transfers. Most of these former POWs do not or did not talk about their experiences. Mario Turrini only told his children that Hawaii was nice, with no comment on his service in Greece, Tunisia, or his experiences at the other camps where he was held in the U.S.

Some of these letters come from Italy and Germany, but some also come from England, Australia, and the United States where these men took their families after the war.

These memories can assist us in planning for the future, promoting the preservation of photos and artifacts from the POW camps. Preservation of these memories can also be achieved by conducting interviews of surviving former POWs, their guards, and members of the community.

We can use these memories and memorabilia to educate public about the policies and experiences of WWII and to promote the good treatment of future POWs.

This photo was taken at the 2009 reunion at Camp Hereford (TX). The U.S. Army is on the left, the former POWs center, and the Italian Air Force on the right. Photo by John Saffell of these men in front of the Chapel built by Italian POWs.

Above: A belt buckle and lariat created for a reunion at Camp Atlanta (NE). (*Gary Reeves' collection of POW artifacts*)

The organization of former POWs in Italy used their old POW ID photos on their membership cards. These groups arranged reunions in Italy and at their former camps in America. Vincenzo Lo Giudice's card was provided by his daughter, Carmelina.

Former POW's Remember

Howard Noel, Channel 5 News — Joe Giordana — Gene Maconi

Gene Maconi and Joe Giordana took time this week to recount stories of the Italian POW camp which later became a service organization located here during World War II. Channel 5 News stopped by to film the occasion as sites of the old facilities were remembered. Mr. Maconi is the operator of a tile company in Ogden and Mr. Giordana is a Depot employee assigned to the Directorate of Installation Services. Both Mr. Maconi and Mr. Giordana went back to Italy after the war but returned to Ogden to make their homes. Asked why they came back both had the same answer – "To marry a local girl."

German ex-soldier visits POW camp

It's a long, long way to Tipperary and to Anzio (Italy) from Dubois, Wyoming.

Corporal Fritz Hartung of the German paratroopers was captured by the Americans in 1943 while defending a strategic pass near Anzio. The next two years he refers to as the best of his life.

The 22-year old German soldier spent two summers and a winter working in a saw mill on Spruce Creek in the Union Pass area near Dubois.

Last week he brought his family back to see what remains of the lumber camp. Norm Wannecke and Arden Coad of Dubois went along to help find the exact location.

Hartung remembered many characteristics of the land. They soon found the camp with a handmade water wheel and troughs still pretty much intact. Various tent and cabin sites are discernible.

Forty POW's, including Hartung, built the camp. At one point there were 120 POW's working as lumberjacks out the Spruce Creek head quarters. The recent forest fire came close to the site, but it was spared.

There were good times, said the ex-POW on his first return to the Dubois area since the war. Although his country was still at war with the United States, he never was mistreated or ridiculed.

The food was excellent in camp. POW's ate with the civilian loggers. Until, that is, about six months before the war's end when the army took over the job of supplying food. Army rations, he found, were not on a par with the other.

Although the POW's were technically prisoners and were under guard, the atmosphere was relaxed. Fritz ran a saw. He remembers the late Martin Olson of Dubois well, because Olson was helpful in showing him how to use the tools.

Hartung joins many area people in recalling good times at Mabel's bar on Long Creek, long ago destroyed by fire and explosion. The civilian camp bosses ignored regulations and took their prisoners to Mabel's for an occasional night on the town.

He does not remember specific names, but recalls that local ranchers brought supplies to the camp. Local civilians often rode up horseback to see what was going on.

At the end of the war, Hartung was sent to England. Since his home in Germany fell under Russian occupation, he decided against repatriation and remained in England. There he met and married Edna, who then immigrated with him to Canada.

Their home is now in Winnipeg where he is a painting contractor. They have five sons and two daughters. Katrina, 9, and Shirley, 11, accompanied them on the week's trip to Dubois.

Fritz finally made it back to Germany about five years ago. He is a Canadian citizen.

For thirty years he has treasured his pictures of the Dubois area and has used them to recall pleasant memories of his POW lumberjack days.

On Friday afternoon time stood still for Fritz Hartung as he relived those "best years of my life".

VISITING POW CAMP... Ex-German POW Fritz Hartung and his daughters examine a water wheel at the site of the World War II camp near Union Pass.

Above left: Photo of TV interview of Joe Giordana and Gene Miconi about their POW years in Utah ASF Depot. (*Courtesy of Special Collections Department, Stewart Library, Weber State University*)

Above right: This newspaper article shows the return of a former POW to Dubois to show his family where he worked as a POW.

Right: Wilson Longo (named for Woodrow Wilson) was born and died in Bellosguardo, Italy. He was a prisoner at Utah ASF Depot. His cousin, Barbara, provided this photo and information.

Below: Mary Ravarino with photos and letters from the Italian POWs from Utah ASF Depot, who worked on her family's farm in Salt Lake City area. (*Italian Center of the West, UtahCulturalNews.com*)

POW Camps by Location

There were 1,204 prisoner of war camps, Italian Service Unit camps, and prisoner of war hospitals in the U.S.

The camp lists at NARA shows several APO addresses in place of camp names. Judging by the dates, these were located in the Philippines, Hawaii, and New Caledonia.

In Montana, there were over 8,800 German, no Italian, and no Japanese POWS in twenty-one POW camps and hospitals. Every one of these locations was a branch camp under Rupert, Idaho as shown in the following list:

Ballantine, Yellowstone County, MT (branch camp under Rupert, ID) opened in October 1944. The maximum population was 555 German POWs in November 1945 doing agricultural work.

Billings, Yellowstone County, MT (branch camp under Rupert, ID) opened in June 1944. The maximum population was 678 German POWs in November 1945 doing agricultural work.

Bridger, Carbon County, MT (branch camp under Rupert, ID) opened in June 1945. The maximum population was 200 German POWs in June 1945 doing agricultural work.

Chinook, Blaine County, MT (branch camp under Rupert, ID) opened in October 1944. The maximum population was 500 German POWs in June 1945 doing agricultural work.

Forsyth, Rosebud County, MT (branch camp under Rupert, ID) opened in October 1944. The maximum population was 569 German POWs in November 1945 doing agricultural work.

Glasgow Army Airfield, Valley County, MT (branch camp under Rupert, ID), now Glasgow International Airport. The camp opened in October 1944. The maximum population was 450 German POWs in October 1945 doing agricultural work.

Glendive, Dawson County, MT (branch camp under Rupert, ID) opened in October 1945. The maximum population was 223 German POWs in October 1945.

Great Falls, Cascade, MT (branch camp under Rupert, ID) opened in November 1945. The maximum population was two German POWs in November 1945.

Hardin No. 1, Big Horn County, MT (branch camp under Rupert, ID) opened in October 1944. The maximum population was 275 German POWs in October 1944 doing agricultural work.

Hardin No. 2, Big Horn County, MT (branch camp under Rupert, ID) (see Holly) opened in June 1945. The maximum population was 2,008 German POWs in November 1945 doing agricultural work.

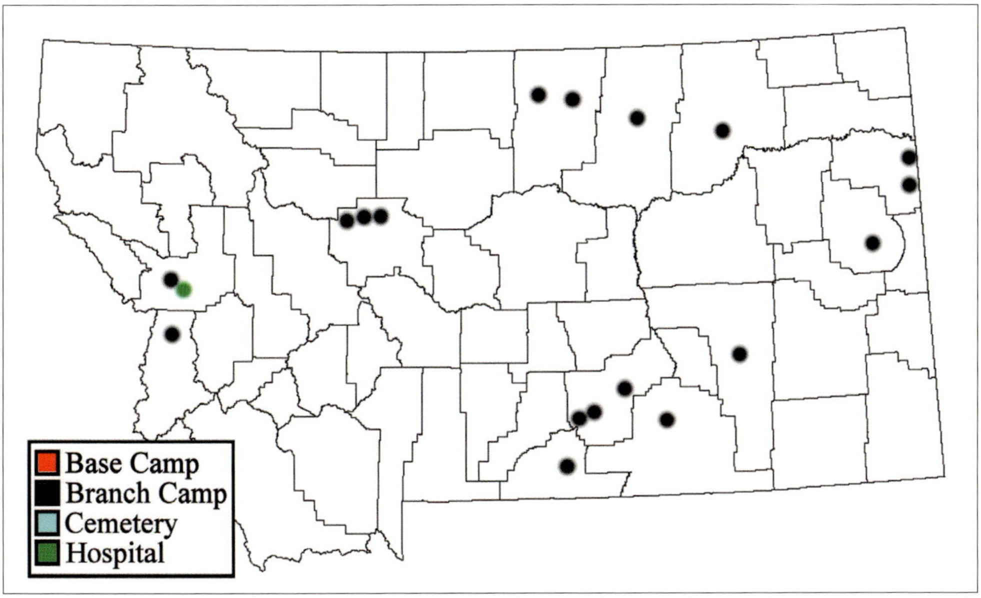

Map showing POW camps and hospitals in Montana. (*John Saffell*)

Harlem, Blaine County, MT (branch camp under Rupert, ID) opened in January 1945. The maximum population was 250 German POWs in January 1945 doing agricultural work.

Holly, Big Horn County, MT (branch camp under Rupert, ID) (see Hardin No. 2).

Laurel, Yellowstone County, MT (branch camp under Rupert, ID) opened in October 1944. The maximum population was 266 German POWs in June 1945 doing agricultural work.

Malta, Phillips County, MT (branch camp under Rupert, ID) opened in June 1945. The maximum population was 300 German POWs in June 1945 doing agricultural work.

Miles City, Custer County, MT (branch camp under Rupert, ID) opened in October 1944. The maximum population was 300 German POWs in June 1945 doing agricultural work.

Missoula (Fort) Hospital, Missoula, Missoula County, MT (branch camp under Rupert, ID) opened in November 1945. The maximum population was one German POW listed as a worker, but more likely a patient in November 1945.

Ridgelawn, Richland County, MT (branch camp under Rupert, ID) opened in October 1945. The maximum population was 333 German POWs in October 1945.

Shaw (Fort), Cascade County, MT (branch camp under Rupert, ID) opened in June 1945. The maximum population was 234 German POWs in June 1945 doing agricultural work.

Sidney, Richland County, MT (branch camp under Rupert, ID) opened in October 1944. The maximum population was 554 German POWs in November 1945 doing agricultural work.

Stevensville, Ravalli County, MT (branch camp under Rupert, ID) opened in October 1945. The maximum population was 260 German POWs in November 1945.

Tucker Crossing, Missoula County, MT (branch camp under Rupert, ID) opened in November 1945. The maximum population was 349 German POWs in June 1946.

Vaughn, Cascade County, MT (branch camp under Rupert, ID) opened in October 1945. The maximum population was 276 German POWs in October 1945.

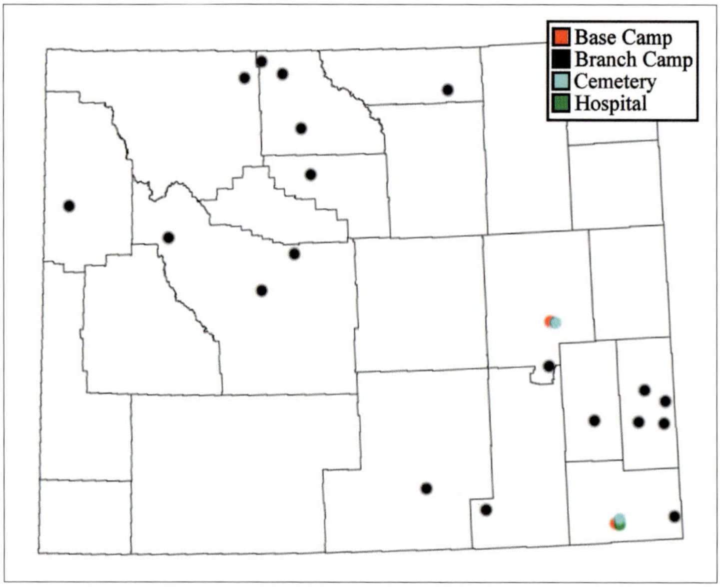

Map showing POW camps and hospitals in Wyoming. (*John Saffell*)

In Wyoming, there were over 12,000 German, over 2,000 Italian, and no Japanese POWs in twenty-two POW camps and hospitals as follows:

Basin, Big Horn County, WY (branch camp under Douglas, later under Scottsbluff) opened in October 1944. The maximum population was 346 German POWs in October 1945 doing agricultural work.

Beaver Creek, Teton County, WY (branch camp under Douglas) opened in September 1945. The maximum population was 245 German POWs in September 1945.

Centennial, Albany County, WY (branch camp under Greeley, CO) opened in August 1945. The maximum population was 275 German POWs in September 1945.

Clearmont, Sheridan County, WY (branch camp under Douglas) opened in June 1945. The maximum population was 253 German POWs in July 1945 doing agricultural work.

Deaver, Big Horn County, WY (branch camp under Douglas) opened in June 1944. The maximum population was 322 German POWs in October 1945 doing agricultural work, primarily harvesting sugar beets.

Douglas (Camp), Douglas, Converse County, WY (base camp), across the river from Wyoming State Fairgrounds opened in February 1944. The maximum population was 1919 Italian POWs in February 1944, followed by 3542 German POWs in May 1945. The work was described as military, although the local memories include the men working on local ranches and farms. Murals on the walls of the Officers' Club have survived due to the efforts of the Independent Order of Odd Fellows Lodge #15, who maintained the building. That building is now a museum for the POW Camp. The artists were Italian POWs who signed their work as V. Finotti, E. Tarquinio, and F. DeRossi.

Douglas #2, Douglas, Converse County, WY (branch camp under Scottsbluff, NE) opened in December 1945. The maximum population was 3,357 German POWs in December 1945 doing military and agricultural work. This was probably a temporary tent camp since there wasn't room at Douglas to double that population.

Above left: Camp Douglas. (*Betty Alberts*)

Above right: The sign at Camp Douglas, located at Wyoming State Archives. (*Department of State Parks and Cultural Resources website*)

Below: Camp Douglas Museum, the former Officers Club at Camp Douglas. (*Author's collection*)

Above and next three pages: Camp Douglas Museum, the former officers' club at Camp Douglas, has murals painted by Italian POWs on many of the walls. (*Author's collection*)

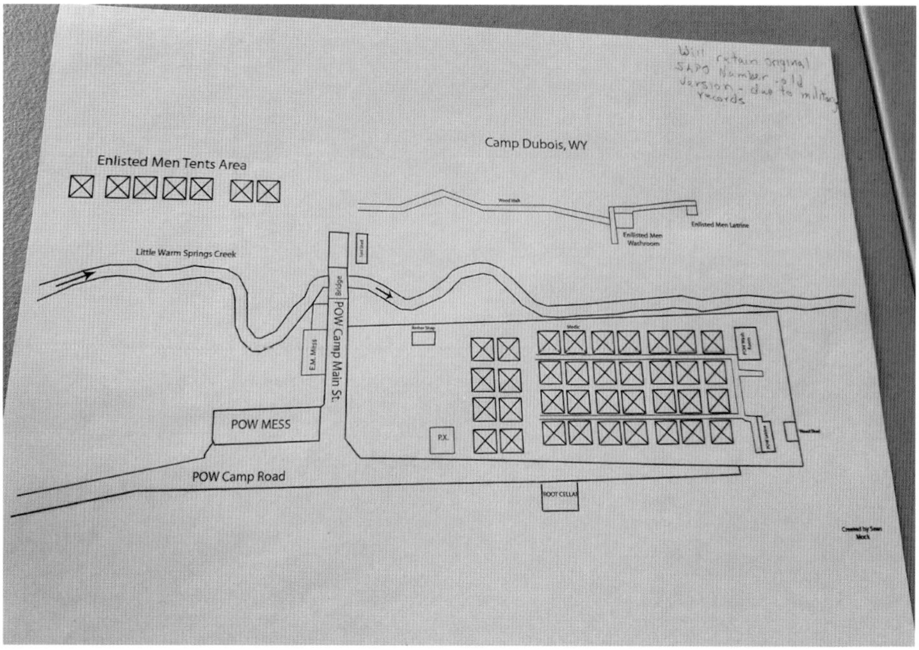

The plan for Camp Dubois. (*Dubois Museum*)

Camp Dubois. (*Dubois Museum*)

Right: This waterwheel provided electricity in the tents at Camp Dubois. (*Dubois Museum*)

Below: Prisoners of war at Camp Dubois. (*Dubois Museum*)

Dubois, Fremont County, WY (branch camp under Scottsbluff, NE) (see Wind River) opened in July 1944. The maximum population was 140 German POWs in October 1944 doing agricultural and forestry work. The POW labor was contracted by the Wyoming Tie and Timber Company to make and transport (by floating, called a "tie drive") railroad ties down the Wind River to Riverton to be processed with creosote before installation along railroad lines. This was the last "tie drive," a procedure used since 1915 and after 1945 replaced by truck transportation. There is an extraordinary PBS documentary of the 1945 tie drive, including film of the POWs at work moving the ties into and down the river. The video is called "Wind River Tie Drive" and is available at the Dubois Museum.

Esterbrook, Converse County, WY (branch camp under Douglas) opened in June 1945. The maximum population was ninety-four German POWs doing work called agricultural in the PMGO reports, but the memories of the area report it was another location for timber work by POWs.

Huntley, Goshen County, WY (branch camp under Scottsbluff, NE) opened in October 1945. The maximum population was 214 German POWs in November 1945.

Lingle, Goshen County, WY (branch camp under Scottsbluff, NE) opened in June 1945. The maximum population was 290 German POWs in November 1945 doing agricultural work.

Lovell, Big Horn County, WY (branch camp under Douglas) opened in June 1945. The maximum population was 200 German POWs in October 1945 doing agricultural work.

Pine Bluffs, Laramie County, WY (branch camp under Scottsbluff, NE) opened in October 1944. The maximum population was 189 German POWs in October 1945 doing agricultural work. The current 4H building is the only remaining structure from the camp.

Powell, Park County, WY (branch camp under Douglas) opened October 1945. The maximum population was 44 German POWs in October 1945.

Regional Hospital, WY (at Fort Warren) opened in September 1944. The maximum population was 10 German POWs in September 1944. This small number indicates that they were patients, not workers.

Riverton, Fremont County, WY (branch camp under Douglas) opened in June 1945. The maximum population was 250 German POWs in June 1945 doing agricultural work.

Ryan Park, Saratoga, Carbon County, WY (branch camp under Greeley, CO) opened in February 1944. The maximum population was 201 Italian POWs in June 1944, followed by 387 German POWs in November 1944. This camp was used by POWs providing labor for timber harvesting.

Torrington, Goshen County, WY (branch camp under Scottsbluff, NE) opened in July 1944. The maximum population was 589 German POWs in October 1944.

Veteran, Goshen County, WY (branch camp under Scottsbluff, NE) opened in May 1944. The maximum population was 244 Italian POWs in June 1944, followed by 423 German POWs in November 1945 doing agricultural work.

Warren (Fort Francis E.), Cheyenne, Laramie County, WY (base camp), now Francis E. Warren Air Force Base, an active military installation. The POW camp opened in February 1944. The maximum population was 803 German POWs in September 1945 doing work classified as military, probably support services for the airfield at this location.

Wheatland, Platte county, WY (branch camp under Douglas) opened in June 1944. The maximum population was 259 German POWs in June 1945 doing agricultural work.

Wind River, Fremont County, WY (branch camp under Scottsbluff, NE) (see Dubois)

Worland, Washakie County, WY (branch camp under Douglas) opened in June 1944. The maximum population was 394 German POWs in October 1945.

Death Index

A total of 880 Germans (includes three Russians, four Austrians, one Yugoslavian, one Czech and one Turk), 172 Italians, twenty-three Japanese (including one Korean) out of 1,076 POWs who died while held in the U.S. during WWI and WWII. Sixteen men died or were buried in Wyoming while POWs. There were no deaths or burials in Montana.

Cavericci, Domenico died of an intestinal obstruction on December 12, 1945, at Fort Warren, WY.

Greco, Giacomo died March 6, 1944, at Fitzsimmons General Hospital, CO, buried at Camp Douglas, WY, transferred to Fort Riley, KS. The captain received full military honors at his funeral at Camp Douglas, including firing squad, bugler, and music by the Italian singers at the camp. His coffin was draped with the Italian flag, according to *The Douglas Budget*, March 16, 1944.

Guenther, Helmut (Helmet) born May 15, 1922, died September 19, 1944, at Fitzsimmons General Hospital, CO, buried at Camp Douglas, WY, transferred to Fort Riley, KS.

Halbig, Peter died November 4, 1944, at Deadman Mountain, CO (a branch camp under Camp Greeley, CO), buried at Fort Warren, WY.

Hoeletzeder, Leopold died August 25, 1944, buried at Fort Warren, WY.

Kuehr, David died July 1, 1945, buried at Fort Warren, WY.

Michel, Jakob born December 23, 1910, at Neckarsteinach, died December 23, 1945, and buried at Fort Warren, WY.

Mueller, Karl died June 28, 1945, buried at Fort Warren, WY.

Nachfeerg, Josef born August 4, 1914, died May 11, 1945, at Fitzsimmons General Hospital, CO, buried at Camp Douglas, WY, transferred to Fort Riley, KS.

Ragozzo, Sabastiano...died May 27, 1944, at Fitzsimmons General Hospital, CO, buried at Camp Douglas, WY, transferred to Fort Riley, KS.

Schneider, Friedrich born July 19, 1924, died July 26, 1944, at Fitzsimmons General Hospital, CO, buried at Camp Douglas, WY, transferred to Fort Riley, KS.

Schweizer, Georg died November 23, 1944, of a logging accident at Ryan Park (a branch camp under Greeley, CO), and was buried at Fort Warren, WY.

Stoll, Max born October 4, 1926, in Himmelkron, died August 28, 1945, at Dubois, WY (a branch camp under Scottsbluff, NE), was buried at Fort Robinson, NE, later transferred with others in that POW cemetery to Camp Butler National Cemetery, IL.

Weiner, Hugo Willi born April 1, 1922, died July 18, 1944, at Fitzsimmons General Hospital, CO, buried at Camp Douglas, WY, transferred to Fort Riley, KS.

Wertititis, Franz died October 27, 1944, buried at Fort Warren, WY.

Winter, Ludwig born March 23, 1909, in Vienna, died May 6, 1945, at Camp Greeley, CO, buried at Fort Warren, WY.

Burial Locations List

A total of ninety-one U.S. Military and civilian cemeteries contained POW burials in the United States.

Places of Burial in Wyoming

Fort Douglas Cemetery, Douglas, WY (four German and two Italian WWII POW burials transferred to Fort Riley, KS on January 24, 1946)
Fort Francis E. Warren Post Cemetery, WY, an active military installation. The cemetery contains eight German and one Italian WWII POW burials outside the walls, but inside the fence, of the cemetery.

Appendix A

POW Labor

MAN-MONTHS SUMMARY OF PRISONER-OF-WAR LABOR

A man-months (strength) summary of prisoner-of-war labor availability, assignment to paid work, and type of work performed, are given in the table and chart below. These data are for all prisoners in the United States except those in Italian Service Units, penal and medical institutions, and Hawaii. Man-months of prisoners available for paid work and prisoners at work are calculated by dividing the total number of man-days so reported by the number of workdays in the month. These man-months data represent average prisoner strength for the month.

MAN-MONTHS OF PRISONER-OF-WAR LABOR, BY TYPE OF WORK AND BY MONTH, NOVEMBER AND DECEMBER 1944, AND JANUARY AND FEBRUARY 1945

Item	Nov 1944	Dec 1944	Jan 1945	Feb 1945
AVAILABILITY AND ASSIGNMENT				
TOTAL MAN-MONTHS a/	306,542	318,034	316,824	318,562
NOT AVAILABLE FOR PAID WORK	95,181	89,862	95,806	95,681
AVAILABLE FOR PAID WORK	211,361	228,172	221,018	222,881
Not Assigned to Work	25,564	34,392	30,074	23,819
Assigned to Work	185,797	193,780	190,944	199,062
Work Stoppage b/	16,273	22,020	19,139	18,559
Worked Full Time	169,524	171,760	171,805	180,503
TYPE OF PAID WORK				
TOTAL MAN-MONTHS	169,524	171,760	171,805	180,503
Prisoner-of-War Camp Work	27,212	28,975	27,810	28,090
Army Post, Camp, and Station Work	85,281	96,915	102,831	112,711
Contract Work	57,031	45,870	41,164	39,702

a/ Calculated from total man-days. Excludes prisoners of war in Italian Service Units, penal and medical institutions, and the Territory of Hawaii.
b/ Average number of men assigned to work but idle each workday during the month because of bad weather, non-use by contract employer, and other temporary causes of work stoppage.

MAN-MONTHS AVAILABLE FOR LABOR, AND TYPE OF WORK DONE BY PRISONERS OF WAR*

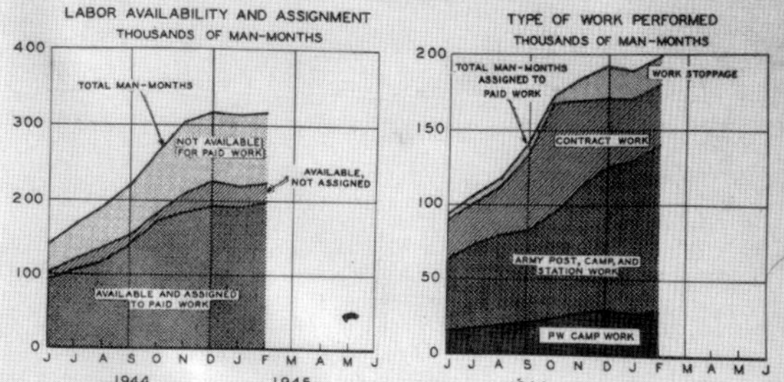

* Excludes prisoners in Italian Service Units, institutions, and Hawaii.

42 RESTRICTED

DECLASSIFIED Authority NND 790120

Next 5 pages: POW work images. (*PMGO, located at NARA College Park, MD, RG 389*)

MOTOR MAINTENANCE

FT. DIX, N. J.

FORT ROBINSON, NEB.

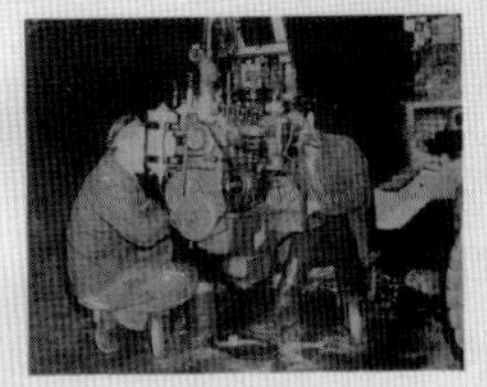

FORT KNOX, KY.

FORT DIX, N. J.

CAMP CAMPBELL, KY.

FT. BRAGG, N. C.

PRISONERS OF WAR WORK

REPAIRS AND UTILITIES

FOLLOWING LIST OF SUGGESTED REPAIRS AND UTILITIES OCCUPATIONS FOR PRISONERS OF WAR WAS PREPARED BY OFFICE OF THE CHIEF OF ENGINEERS

SPECIFICATION NUMBER OCCUPATION

CAMP CLARK, MO.

FORT OGELTHORPE, GA.

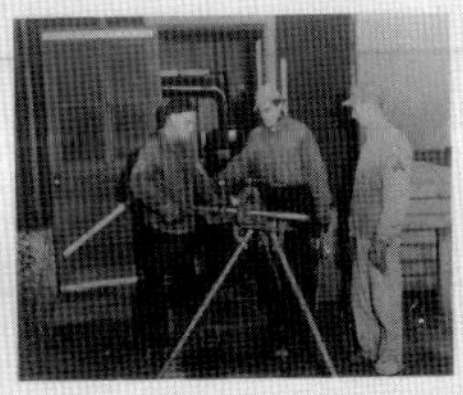

CAMP CLARK, MO.

FORT LEONARD WOOD, MO.

TAILOR, CLOTHING REPAIR SHOP

COBBLERS, SHOE REPAIR SHOP

MECHANIC, TYPEWRITER REPAIR SHOP

PRISONERS OF WAR

Auto body repairmen
Auto painters
Auto mechanics
Artists
Bakers, bread and pastry
  Mixers
  Oven operators
  Moulders
  Dividers
Barbers
Blacksmiths
Bookkeepers
Boot and shoe repairmen
Boxmakers
Bricklayers
Brushmen
Bulldozer operators
Butchers
Cabinetmakers
Canvas workers
Carpenters
  Bench
  Car
  Concrete form
  House
  Rough
Car washers and greasers
Cement and concrete finishers
Ceramic workers
Checkers
Chemists
  Sewage disposal plant
Cleaners
  Engine
  Floor
  Machine
Clerks
  General office
  Statistical
  Stock
Clothing classifiers
Clothing repairmen
Coal handlers
Cobblers
Countermen
Concrete workers
Construction machinery operators
Construction laborers
Cooks
  EM mess
  Officers' mess
  PX restaurant
Coppersmiths
Cranemen
Craters
Dairymen
Dental lab. workers
Ditch diggers
Draftsmen
Dragline operators
Dyers
Electrical repairmen
Electricians
  Auto
  House
  Motor
  Radio
Engravers
Fan cleaners
Farm hands
Farm machinery operators
Firemen
  Boiler and furnace
  Fire department
Form builders
Flashlight repairmen
Freight handlers
Furnace cleaners
Furnace tenders
Furniture repairmen
Foundry workers
Garbage laborers
Garbage collectors
Gardners
Glaziers
Goldsmiths
Graders and packers
  Fruit and vegetable
Grass mowers
Grave diggers
Greenhouse workers
Grounds keepers
Harness makers
Harvest hands
  Cotton
  Fruit
  General
  Sugar beets
  Sugarcane
  Tobacco
  Vegetable
Hospital orderlies
Incinerator operators
Insect exterminators
Interpreters
Instrument repairmen
Irrigation workers
Janitors
Jewelers
Kitchen police
Laborer, general
Language teachers
Latrine orderlies
Laundry workers
  Checker
  Marker
  Presser
  Sorter
  Washer
Leather workers
Locksmiths
Lumberyard workers
Machinists
Masons
Meatcutters
Mechanics

OCCUPATIONS AND SKILLS OF

PRISONERS OF WAR (Continued)

Maintenance workers:
  Ditches
  Grounds
  Powerline right-of-way
  Railroad right-of-way
  Roads and streets
  Septic tanks
Model and pattern makers
Molders
Motor repairmen
  Electrical
  Gasoline and diesel
Nurserymen
Office-machine repairmen
Oilers
Orthopedic aids
Painters
  Construction
  Maintenance
  Vehicle
Paper balers
Photograph finishers
Photographers' assistants
Physicians
Piano tuners
Pinboys
Plasterers
Printers
Plumbers
Poultry dressers
Pulpwood cutters
Quarry workers
Radio repairmen
Ration breakdown workers
Repairmen
  Automobile
  Clothing
  Electrical
  Furniture
  Instrument
  Motor
  Office machine
  Radio
  Road equipment
  Shoe
  Tent
  Tire
  Typewriter
  Watch
Railroad maintenance workers
Refrigeration mechanics
Road equipment repairmen
Roofers
Salvage workers:
  Building materials
  Clothing and equipment
  Electrical equipment
  Motors
  Paper
Saw filers
Sawmill workers
Scrubmen
Servicemen, motor pool
Sheet metal workers
Sewage disposal plant operators
Shoe classifiers
Shoe repairmen
Sign painters
Silversmiths
Spray operators
  Mosquito control
  Tree spraying
Stablemen
Steam cleaners
  Vehicles
Steam fitters
Stonecutters
Stone masons
Storekeepers
Sweepers
Tailors
Teachers
Teamsters
Telephone linemen
Tent repairmen
Textile balers
Tile setters
Timekeepers
Tinsmiths
Tire changers
Tire repairmen
Tool checkers and sorters
Tool dressers and sharpeners
Track repairmen
Tree fellers
Tractor drivers
Truck drivers
Type setters
Typewriter repairmen
Typists
Upholsterers
  Furniture
  Vehicles
Veterinarians
Waiters
  EM mess
  Officers' club
  PX restaurant
Ward boys
  Station hospital
Warehousemen
  Post ordnance
  Post quartermaster
  Salvage shop
  Post exchange
  Private industry
Wash-rack man
Watch repairmen
Water plant operators
Weavers
  Basketry
Webbing repairmen
Welders
Woodsmen
Wood workers
X-ray lab. technicians
Yardmen

MECHANICS, VEHICLE REPAIR SHOP

AUTO PAINTER, VEHICLE REPAIR SHOP

PLUMBERS, POST PLUMBING SHOP

PRISONERS OF WAR WORK

POST ENGINEER WORK

CAMP TRINIDAD, COLO.

CAMP SHELBY, MISS.

FORT LEONARD WOOD, MO.

CAMP BRECKINRIDGE, KY.

CAMP BRECKINRIDGE, KY.

CAMP WHEELER, GA.

WD - ASF - PMGO

PRISONERS OF WAR WORK

POST ENGINEER WORK

CAMP CLINTON, MISS.

CAMP SUTTON, N. C.

EDGEWOOD ARSENAL, MD.

CAMP CARSON, COLO.

GALVESTON AAB, TEX.

FORT LEONARD WOOD, MO.

WD - ASF - PMGO

PRISONERS OF WAR WORK

POST ENGINEER WORK

FORT BENJAMIN HARRISON, IND.

CAMP BRECKINRIDGE, KY.

NORFOLK ARMY AIR BASE, VA.

CAMP CLINTON, MISS.

FORT DEVENS, MASS.

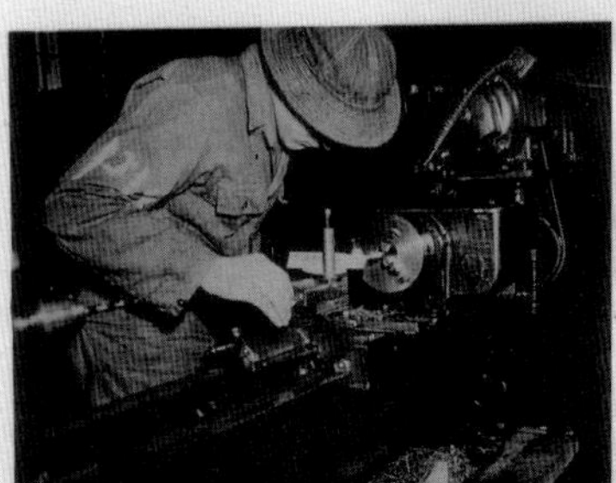

CAMP LEE, VA.

WD - ASF - PMGO

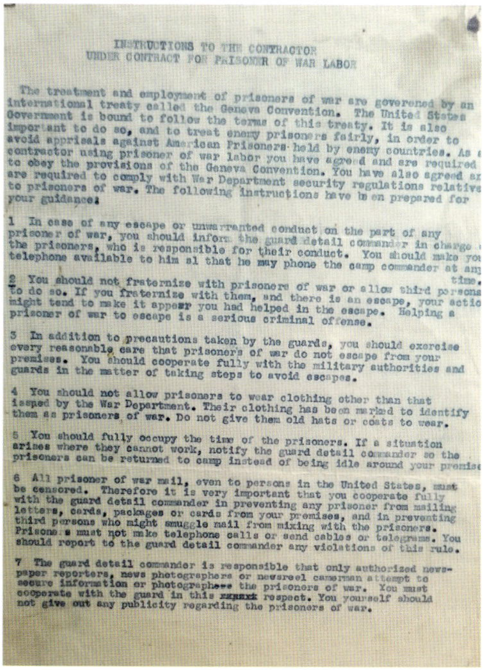

INSTRUCTIONS TO THE CONTRACTOR
UNDER CONTRACT FOR PRISONER OF WAR LABOR

The treatment and employment of prisoners of war are governed by an international treaty called the Geneva Convention. The United States Government is bound to follow the terms of this treaty. It is also important to do so, and to treat enemy prisoners fairly, in order to avoid apprisals against American Prisoners held by enemy countries. As a contractor using prisoner of war labor you have agreed and are required to obey the provisions of the Geneva Convention. You have also agreed and are required to comply with War Department security regulations relative to prisoners of war. The following instructions have been prepared for your guidance:

1 In case of any escape or unwarranted conduct on the part of any prisoner of war, you should inform the guard detail commander in charge of the prisoners, who is responsible for their conduct. You should make your telephone available to him so that he may phone the camp commander at any time.

2 You should not fraternize with prisoners of war or allow third persons to do so. If you fraternize with them, and there is an escape, your action might tend to make it appear you had helped in the escape. Helping a prisoner of war to escape is a serious criminal offense.

3 In addition to precautions taken by the guards, you should exercise every reasonable care that prisoners of war do not escape from your premises. You should cooperate fully with the military authorities and guards in the matter of taking steps to avoid escapes.

4 You should not allow prisoners to wear clothing other than that issued by the War Department. Their clothing has been marked to identify them as prisoners of war. Do not give them old hats or coats to wear.

5 You should fully occupy the time of the prisoners. If a situation arises where they cannot work, notify the guard detail commander so the prisoners can be returned to camp instead of being idle around your premises.

6 All prisoner of war mail, even to persons in the United States, must be censored. Therefore it is very important that you cooperate fully with the guard detail commander in preventing any prisoner from mailing letters, cards, packages or cards from your premises, and in preventing third persons who might smuggle mail from mixing with the prisoners. Prisoners must not make telephone calls or send cables or telegrams. You should report to the guard detail commander any violations of this rule.

7 The guard detail commander is responsible that only authorized newspaper reporters, news photographers or newsreel cameraman attempt to secure information or photographs the prisoners of war. You must cooperate with the guard in this respect. You yourself should not give out any publicity regarding the prisoners of war.

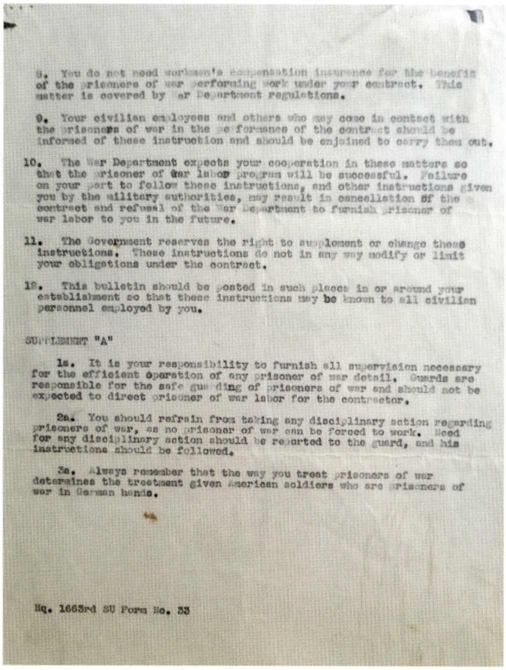

8. You do not need workmen's compensation insurance for the benefit of the prisoners of war performing work under your contract. This matter is covered by War Department regulations.

9. Your civilian employees and others who may come in contact with the prisoners of war in the performance of the contract should be informed of these instruction and should be enjoined to carry them out.

10. The War Department expects your cooperation in these matters so that the prisoner of war labor program will be successful. Failure on your part to follow these instructions, and other instructions given you by the military authorities, may result in cancellation of the contract and refusal of the War Department to furnish prisoner of war labor to you in the future.

11. The Government reserves the right to supplement or change these instructions. These instructions do not in any way modify or limit your obligations under the contract.

12. This bulletin should be posted in such places in or around your establishment so that these instructions may be known to all civilian personnel employed by you.

SUPPLEMENT "A"

1a. It is your responsibility to furnish all supervision necessary for the efficient operation of any prisoner of war detail. Guards are responsible for the safe guarding of prisoners of war and should not be expected to direct prisoner of war labor for the contractor.

2a. You should refrain from taking any disciplinary action regarding prisoners of war, as no prisoner of war can be forced to work. Need for any disciplinary action should be reported to the guard, and his instructions should be followed.

3a. Always remember that the way you treat prisoners of war determines the treatment given American soldiers who are prisoners of war in German hands.

Hq. 1663rd SU Form No. 33

Above: POW contract instructions. (Gary Reeves' collection of POW artifacts)

Below: POW labor in Sixth Service Command. (*Gary Reeves' collection of POW artifacts*)

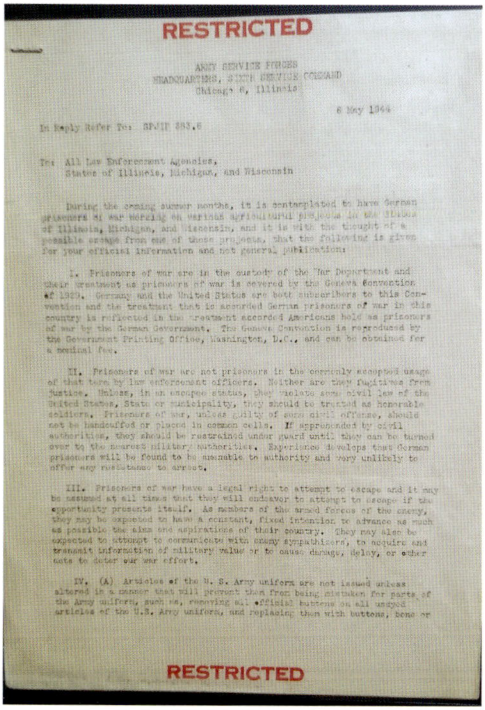

RESTRICTED

ARMY SERVICE FORCES
HEADQUARTERS, SIXTH SERVICE COMMAND
Chicago 6, Illinois

6 May 1944

In Reply Refer To: SPJIP 383.6

To: All Law Enforcement Agencies,
States of Illinois, Michigan, and Wisconsin

During the coming summer months, it is contemplated to have German prisoners of war working on various agricultural projects in the States of Illinois, Michigan, and Wisconsin, and it is with the thought of a possible escape from one of these projects, that the following is given for your official information and not general publication:

I. Prisoners of war are in the custody of the War Department and their treatment as prisoners of war is covered by the Geneva Convention of 1929. Germany and the United States are both subscribers to this Convention and the treatment that is accorded German prisoners of war in this country is reflected in the treatment accorded Americans held as prisoners of war by the German Government. The Geneva Convention is reproduced by the Government Printing Office, Washington, D.C., and can be obtained for a nominal fee.

II. Prisoners of war are not prisoners in the commonly accepted usage of that term by law enforcement officers. Neither are they fugitives from justice. Unless, in an escapee status, they violate some civil law of the United States, State or municipality, they should be treated as honorable soldiers. Prisoners of war, unless guilty of some civil offense, should not be handcuffed or placed in common cells. If apprehended by civil authorities, they should be restrained under guard until they can be turned over to the nearest military authorities. Experience develops that German prisoners will be found to be amenable to authority and very unlikely to offer any resistance to arrest.

III. Prisoners of war have a legal right to attempt to escape and it may be assumed at all times that they will endeavor to attempt to escape if the opportunity presents itself. As members of the armed forces of the enemy, they may be expected to have a constant, fixed intention to advance as much as possible the aims and aspirations of their country. They may also be expected to attempt to communicate with enemy sympathizers, to acquire and transmit information of military value or to cause damage, delay, or other acts to deter our war effort.

IV. (A) Articles of the U. S. Army uniform are not issued unless altered in a manner that will prevent them from being mistaken for parts of the Army uniform, such as, removing all official buttons on all undyed articles of the U.S. Army uniform, and replacing them with buttons, bone or

RESTRICTED

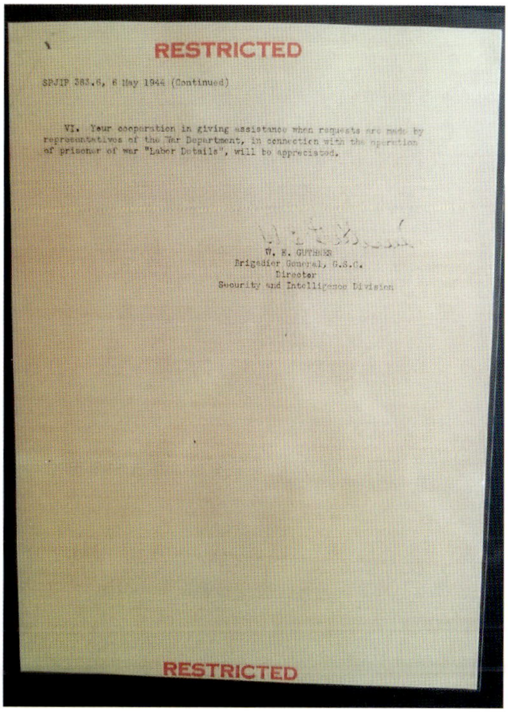

RESTRICTED

SPJIP 383.6, 6 May 1944 (Continued)

VI. Your cooperation in giving assistance when requests are made by representatives of the War Department, in connection with the operation of prisoner of war "Labor Details", will be appreciated.

W. E. GUTHNER
Brigadier General, G.S.C.
Director
Security and Intelligence Division

RESTRICTED

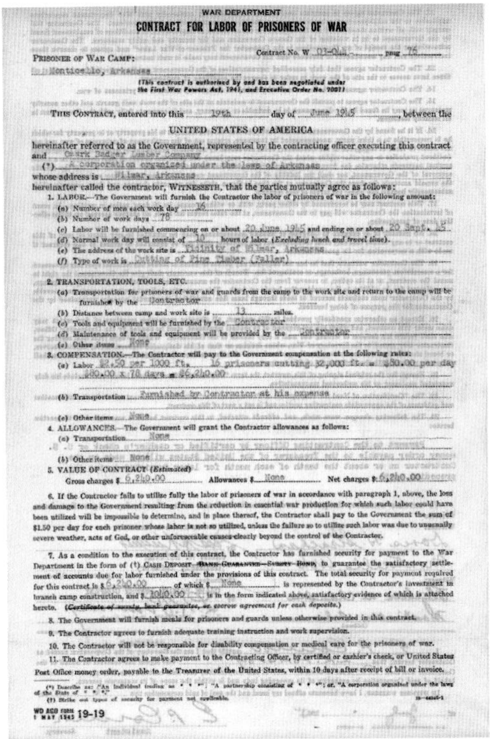

WAR DEPARTMENT

CONTRACT FOR LABOR OF PRISONERS OF WAR

Contract No. W 03-041 pmg 76

PRISONER OF WAR CAMP:
Monticello, Arkansas

(This contract is authorized by and has been negotiated under the First War Powers Act, 1941, and Executive Order No. 9001)

THIS CONTRACT, entered into this 19th day of June 1945, between the

UNITED STATES OF AMERICA

hereinafter referred to as the Government, represented by the contracting officer executing this contract and Ozark Badger Lumber Company
(*) A corporation organized under the laws of Arkansas
whose address is Wilmar, Arkansas
hereinafter called the contractor, WITNESSETH, that the parties mutually agree as follows:

1. LABOR.—The Government will furnish the Contractor the labor of prisoners of war in the following amount:
(a) Number of men each work day 16
(b) Number of work days 78
(c) Labor will be furnished commencing on or about 20 June 1945 and ending on or about 20 Sept. 45
(d) Normal work day will consist of 10 hours of labor *(Excluding lunch and travel time).*
(e) The address of the work site is Vicinity of Wilmar, Arkansas
(f) Type of work is Cutting of Pine Timber (Faller)

2. TRANSPORTATION, TOOLS, ETC.
(a) Transportation for prisoners of war and guards from the camp to the work site and return to the camp will be furnished by the Contractor
(b) Distance between camp and work site is 13 miles.
(c) Tools and equipment will be furnished by the Contractor
(d) Maintenance of tools and equipment will be provided by the Contractor
(e) Other items None

3. COMPENSATION.—The Contractor will pay to the Government compensation at the following rates:
(a) Labor $2.50 per 1000 ft. 16 prisoners cutting 32,000 ft. = $80.00 per day
$80.00 x 78 days = $6,240.00
(b) Transportation Furnished by Contractor at his expense
(c) Other items None

4. ALLOWANCES.—The Government will grant the Contractor allowances as follows:
(a) Transportation None
(b) Other items None

5. VALUE OF CONTRACT *(Estimated)*
Gross charges $ 6,240.00 Allowances $ None Net charges $ 6,240.00

6. If the Contractor fails to utilize fully the labor of prisoners of war in accordance with paragraph 1, above, the loss and damage to the Government resulting from the reduction in essential war production for which such labor could have been utilized will be impossible to determine, and in place thereof, the Contractor shall pay to the Government the sum of $1.50 per day for each prisoner whose labor is not so utilized, unless the failure so to utilize such labor was due to unusually severe weather, acts of God, or other unforeseeable causes clearly beyond the control of the Contractor.

7. As a condition to the execution of this contract, the Contractor has furnished security for payment to the War Department in the form of (†) CASH DEPOSIT ~~BANK GUARANTEE—SURETY BOND~~, to guarantee the satisfactory settlement of accounts due for labor furnished under the provisions of this contract. The total security for payment required for this contract is $ 6,240.00 of which $ None is represented by the Contractor's investment in branch camp construction, and $ 1040.00 is in the form indicated above, satisfactory evidence of which is attached hereto. *(~~Certificate of surety, bank guarantee, or~~ escrow agreement for cash deposits.)*

8. The Government will furnish meals for prisoners and guards unless otherwise provided in this contract.

9. The Contractor agrees to furnish adequate training instruction and work supervision.

10. The Contractor will not be responsible for disability compensation or medical care for the prisoners of war.

11. The Contractor agrees to make payment to the Contracting Officer, by certified or cashier's check, or United States Post Office money order, payable to the Treasurer of the United States, within 10 days after receipt of bill or invoice.

(*) Describe as: "An individual trading as * * *"; "A partnership consisting of * * *"; or, "A corporation organized under the laws of the State of * * *."
(†) Strike out types of security for payment not applicable.

WD AGO FORM 19-19
1 MAY 1945

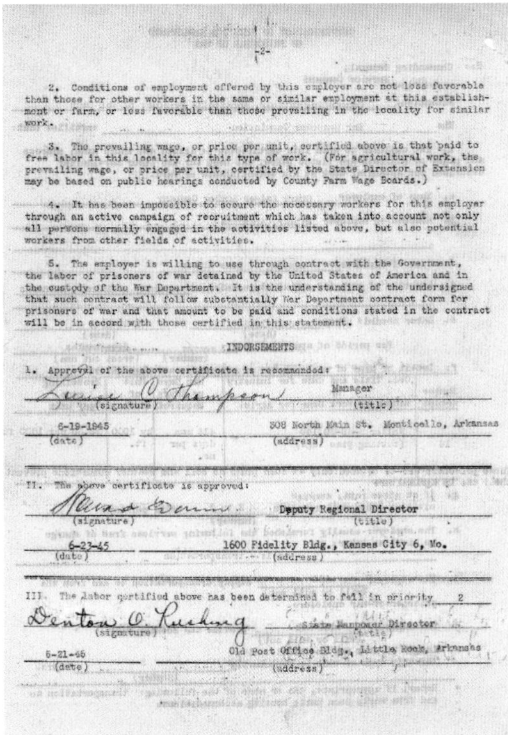

-2-

2. Conditions of employment offered by this employer are not less favorable than those for other workers in the same or similar employment at this establishment or farm, or less favorable than those prevailing in the locality for similar work.

3. The prevailing wage, or price per unit, certified above is that paid to free labor in this locality for this type of work. (For agricultural work, the prevailing wage, or price per unit, certified by the State Director of Extension may be based on public hearings conducted by County Farm Wage Boards.)

4. It has been impossible to secure the necessary workers for this employer through an active campaign of recruitment which has taken into account not only all persons normally engaged in the activities listed above, but also potential workers from other fields of activities.

5. The employer is willing to use through contract with the Government, the labor of prisoners of war detained by the United States of America and in the custody of the War Department. It is the understanding of the undersigned that such contract will follow substantially War Department contract form for prisoners of war and that amount to be paid and conditions stated in the contract will be in accord with those certified in this statement.

INDORSEMENTS

1. Approval of the above certificate is recommended:
Louise C. Thompson (signature) Manager (title)
6-19-1945 (date) 308 North Main St. Monticello, Arkansas (address)

II. The above certificate is approved:
(signature) Deputy Regional Director (title)
6-23-45 (date) 1600 Fidelity Bldg., Kansas City 6, Mo. (address)

III. The labor certified above has been determined to fall in priority 2
Denton O. Rushing (signature) State Manpower Director (title)
6-21-45 (date) Old Post Office Bldg., Little Rock, Arkansas (address)

Work contracts for civilians to obtain POW labor. (*Michael Pomeroy*)

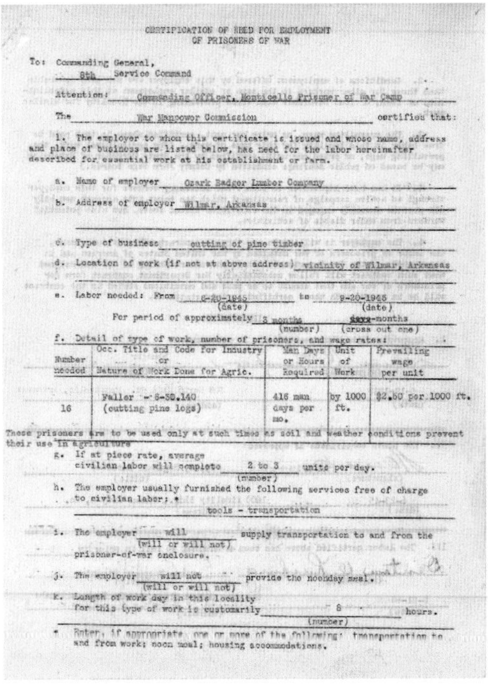

CERTIFICATION OF NEED FOR EMPLOYMENT
OF PRISONERS OF WAR

To: Commanding General,
8th Service Command

Attention: Commanding Officer, Monticello Prisoner of War Camp

The War Manpower Commission certifies that:

1. The employer to whom this certificate is issued and whose name, address and place of business are listed below, has need for the labor hereinafter described for essential work at his establishment or farm.

a. Name of employer Ozark Badger Lumber Company
b. Address of employer Wilmar, Arkansas
c. Type of business cutting of pine timber
d. Location of work (if not at above address) vicinity of Wilmar, Arkansas
e. Labor needed: From 6-20-1945 (date) to 9-20-1945 (date)
For period of approximately 3 months (number) ~~days~~-months (cross out one)
f. Detail of type of work, number of prisoners, and wage rates:

Number needed	Occ. Title and Code for Industry or Nature of Work Done for Agric.	Man Days or Hours Required	Unit of Work	Prevailing wage per unit
16	Faller - 8-30.140 (cutting pine logs)	416 man days per mo.	by 1000 ft.	$2.50 per 1000 ft.

These prisoners are to be used only at such times as soil and weather conditions prevent their use in agriculture

g. If at piece rate, average civilian labor will complete 2 to 3 (number) units per day.
h. The employer usually furnished the following services free of charge to civilian labor: *
tools - transportation
i. The employer will (will or will not) supply transportation to and from the prisoner-of-war enclosure.
j. The employer will not (will or will not) provide the noonday meal.
k. Length of work day in this locality for this type of work is customarily 8 (number) hours.

* Enter, if appropriate, one or more of the following: transportation to and from work; noon meal; housing accommodations.

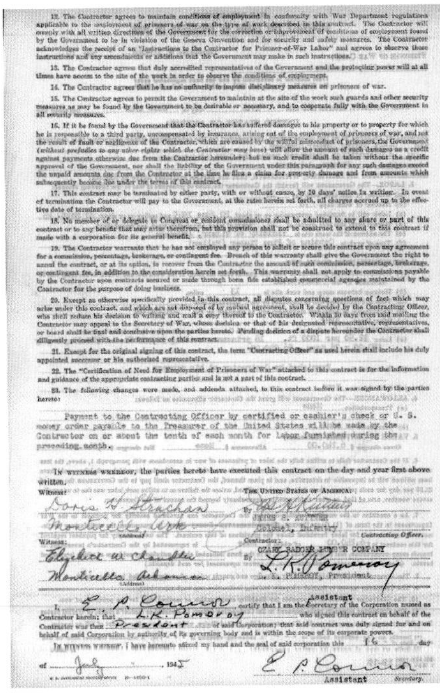

12. The Contractor agrees to maintain conditions of employment in conformity with War Department regulations applicable to the employment of prisoners of war on the type of work described in this contract. The Contractor will comply with all written directions of the Government for the correction or improvement of conditions of employment found by the Government to be in violation of the Geneva Convention and for security and safety measures. The Contractor acknowledges the receipt of an "Instructions to the Contractor for Prisoner-of-War Labor" and agrees to observe those instructions and any amendments or additions that the Government may make in such instructions.

13. The Contractor agrees that duly accredited representatives of the Government and the protecting power will at all times have access to the site of the work in order to observe the conditions of employment.

14. The Contractor agrees that he has no authority to impose disciplinary measures on prisoners of war.

15. The Contractor agrees to permit the Government to maintain at the site of the work such guards and other security measures as may be found by the Government to be desirable or necessary, and to cooperate fully with the Government in all security measures.

16. If it be found by the Government that the Contractor has suffered damages to his property or to property for which he is responsible to a third party, uncompensated by insurance, arising out of the employment of prisoners of war, and not the result of fault or negligence of the Contractor, which are caused by the willful misconduct of prisoners, the Government *(without prejudice to any other rights which the Contractor may have)* will allow the amount of such damages as a credit against payments otherwise due from the Contractor hereunder; but no such credit shall be taken without the specific approval of the Government, nor shall the liability of the Government under this paragraph for any such damages exceed the unpaid amounts due from the Contractor at the time he files a claim for property damage and from amounts which subsequently become due under the terms of this contract.

17. This contract may be terminated by either party, with or without cause, by 10 days' notice in writing. In event of termination the Contractor will pay to the Government, at the rates herein set forth, all charges accrued up to the effective date of termination.

18. No member of or delegate to Congress or resident commissioner shall be admitted to any share or part of this contract or to any benefit that may arise therefrom, but this provision shall not be construed to extend to this contract if made with a corporation for its general benefit.

19. The Contractor warrants that he has not employed any person to solicit or secure this contract upon any agreement for a commission, percentage, brokerage, or contingent fee. Breach of this warranty shall give the Government the right to annul the contract, or at its option, to recover from the Contractor the amount of such commission, percentage, brokerage, or contingent fee, in addition to the consideration herein set forth. This warranty shall not apply to commissions payable by the Contractor upon contracts secured or made through bona fide established commercial agencies maintained by the Contractor for the purpose of doing business.

20. Except as otherwise specifically provided in this contract, all disputes concerning questions of fact which may arise under this contract, and which are not disposed of by mutual agreement, shall be decided by the Contracting Officer, who shall reduce his decision to writing and mail a copy thereof to the Contractor. Within 30 days from said mailing the Contractor may appeal to the Secretary of War, whose decision or that of his designated representative, representatives, or board shall be final and conclusive upon the parties hereto. Pending decision of a dispute hereunder the Contractor shall diligently proceed with the performance of this contract.

21. Except for the original signing of this contract, the term "Contracting Officer" as used herein shall include his duly appointed successor or his authorized representative.

22. The "Certification of Need for Employment of Prisoners of War" attached to this contract is for the information and guidance of the appropriate contracting parties and is not a part of this contract.

23. The following changes were made, and addenda attached, to this contract before it was signed by the parties hereto:

Payment to the Contracting Officer by certified or cashier's check or U. S. money order payable to the Treasurer of the United States will be made by the Contractor on or about the tenth of each month for labor furnished during the preceding month.

IN WITNESS WHEREOF, the parties hereto have executed this contract on the day and year first above written.

Witness: Doris H. Strachan
Monticello, Ark. (Address)

THE UNITED STATES OF AMERICA:
By
Colonel, Infantry
Contracting Officer.

Witness: Elizabeth W. Chandler
Monticello, Arkansas (Address)

Contractor:
OZARK BADGER LUMBER COMPANY
By L. K. Pomeroy
L. K. POMEROY, President

I, E. P. Connor, certify that I am the Assistant Secretary of the Corporation named as Contractor herein; that L.K. Pomeroy who signed this contract on behalf of the Contractor was then President of said Corporation; that said contract was duly signed for and on behalf of said Corporation by authority of its governing body and is within the scope of its corporate powers.

IN WITNESS WHEREOF, I have hereunto affixed my hand and the seal of said corporation this 16 day of July, 1945

E. P. Connor
Assistant *Secretary.*

Appendix B

Museums and Websites

Arizona Historical Society Museum, Papago Park, AZ: arizonahistoricalsociety.org/museums
Billion Graves:billiongraves.com
Camp Aliceville: encyclopediaofalabama.org/face/Article.isp?id-2322.
Camp Hearne Museum: camphearne.com/index.htm
Camp Opelika: eastalabama.org/Exhibits/Exhibits.htm
Camp Ruston: latech.edu/library/scma/index.php
Camp Van Dorn World War II Museum: vandorn.org
Cemetery Records Online: interment.net
Deschutes County Historical Museum, 129 NW Idaho Ave, Bend, OR 97703, deschuteshistory.org
Door County Maritime Museum, Sturgeon Bay, WI has display on WWII POWs in the area orchards
Douglas WWII POW Camp Museum: 115 Riverbend Dr., Douglas, WY 82633-9139, wyoparks.state.wy.us/index.php/activities-amenities-camp-douglas/museum-camp-douglas-officers-club
Drew County Museum, Monticello, AR has a display on WWII POWs at Camp Monticello.
Dubois Museum – 909 W. Ramshorn St., Dubois, WY 82513, fremontcountymuseums.com/
Family Search: familysearch.org
Find a Grave: findagrave.com
Fort Douglas, Salt Lake City, UT: fortdouglas.org/about/virtual-tour, also cemetery
Fort George G. Meade Museum: ftmeade.army.mil/museum/Museum_POW.html
Fort Leonard Wood Museum: visitmo.com/museums-at-fort-leonard-wood.aspx
Fort Missoula Historical Museum – fortmissoulamuseum.org
GenTracer—World War II: gentracer.org
German War Graves Commission: volksbund.de
Library of Congress: catalog.loc.gov
March Field Air Museum, Riverside, CA: marchfield.org
Mississippi Armed Forces Museum, Camp Shelby, MS: armedforcesmuseum.us/Pages/Newsletter.pdf
Mountain Empire Historical Society and Stone Museum, Campo, CA: cssmus.org/
Oregon Historical Society Davies Family Research Library, Portland, OR 97205 has eighty-one photos from the U.S. Army Signal Corps in their archives.
Traces: traces.org
U.K. National Archives: nationalarchives.gov.uk
U.S. Dept. of Veterans Affairs National Cemeteries: cem.va.gov/cem/cems/listcem.asp

U.S. National Archives and Records Administration: archives.gov
U.S. National Park Service: nps.gov
Warren AFB Museum: warrenmuseum.com/
Weber State University, Stewart Library, Special Collections Exhibits, "Prisoners of War in Ogden" at library.weber.edu/collections/special_collections
Wyoming State Archives: wyoarchives.state.wy.us/Admin/About.aspx

Bibliography

Adams, Meredith Lentz. "A Miscarriage of Justice?" interview by Jim Kelly. Sunflower Journeys Home 16101A. KTWU. 2003.

_____. *Murder and Martial Justice: Spying and Retribution in World War II America*. Kent, Ohio: Kent State University Press, 2011.

_____. "The Abortive Attempt to Exchange GI and German POWs". (Presentation, TRACES conference, May 31, 2003).

Alberts, Betty. Interview by author. March 10, 2012.

Amdt, Karl John Richard. "German P.O.W. Camp Papers." Microfilm. Washington, DC: Library of Congress Photo-duplication Service, 1965. Library of Congress. lccn.loc.gov/83125121.

Angerilli, Adriano. Interview by author. August 14 ,2009.

Army Service Forces. "Service Command Operating Personnel and Prisoners, 31 March 1945", NARA RG 389, Entry 261, Box 2563. National Archives at College Park, College Park, MD.

Bangerter, Lowell. *German Prisoners of War in Wyoming*. 1979.

Bland, John Paul. *Secret War at Home: The Pine Grove Furnace Prisoner of War Interrogation Camp*. Cumberland County Historical Society, Carlisle, PA, 2006.

Boni, Andrea. Interview by author. November 3, 2018.

Boudreaux, Henry J, Capt., C.M.P. Report of Investigation of the deaths of Leonello Bini, Vito Clemente, Adolfo Nitri, Antonino Paleologo, July 21, 1943, NARA RG 389, Entry 461, Box 2562. National Archives at College Park, College Park, MD.

Bryan, B.M., Brigadeer General. Assistant Provost Marshal General, Letter to Army Services Forces regarding transfer of POWs, August 26, 1944, NARA RG 389, Entry 457, Box 1419. National Archives at College Park, College Park, MD.

Bulkat, Ernst. Interview by author. March 11, 2007.

Bykofsky, Joseph and Harold Larson. *United States Army in World War II: The Technical Services: The Transportation Corps: Operations Overseas*. Center of Military History, United States Army, Washington, DC, 2003.

Carlson, Lewis. "POW Experience: Myth and Reality". (Presentation, TRACES conference, 6 October 2002).

Conn, Stetson and Byron Fairchild. *The United States Army in World War II, The Western Hemisphere, The Framework of Hemisphere Defense*. Washington, DC: Office of the Chief of Military History, Department of the Army, 1960.

Conn, Stetson and Rose C Engelman and Byron Fairchild, *The United States Army in World War II, The Western Hemisphere, Guarding the United States and its Outposts*. Washington, DC: Office of the Chief of Military History, Department of the Army, 1964

Corbin, Alexander, *The History of Camp Tracy: Japanese WWII POWs and the Future of Strategic Interrogation*. Fort Belvoir, VA: Ziedon Press, 2009

Cosentini, George and Norman Gruenzner. *United States Numbered Military Post Offices Assignments and Locations 1941–1994*. The Military Postal History Society, 1994.

Cowley, Betty. *Stalag Wisconsin: Inside WWII Prisoner-of-war Camps*. Oregon, WI: Badger Books, 2002.

Cunningham, Raymond Kelly. *Prisoners at Fort Douglas: War Prison Barracks Three and the alien enemies, 1917–1920*. Salt Lake City, UT: Fort Douglas Military Museum, 1983.

Daugherty, Joseph B., Col. Assistant, Office of the Quartermaster General, Letter to Provost Marshal General regarding repatriation of ISU units, dated October 9, 1945, NARA RG 389, Entry 261, Box 2563. National Archives and Records Administration, College Park, MD

_____. Letter to Provost Marshal General regarding repatriation of ISU units, dated August 28, 1945, NARA RG 389, Entry 261, Box 2563. National Archives and Records Administration, College Park, MD

"Department of Veterans Affairs National Cemeteries," United States Department of Veterans Affairs, cem.va.gov/cem/cems/listcem.asp.

Ducharme, Joseph O.C., Lt. Col. Director, Enemy PW Information Bureau, Camp Holabird, MD, to Provost Marshal General, regarding cemetery locations, dated February 16, 1953, NARA RG 389, Entry 261, Box 2562. National Archives and Records Administration, College Park, MD

_____. Regarding cemetery locations, dated February 16, 1953, NARA RG 389, Entry 467, Box 1513. National Archives and Records Administration, College Park, MD

Dvorak, Petula. "Fort Hunt's Quiet Men Break Silence on WWII: Interrogator Fought "Battle of Wits."" *The Washington Post*. October 6, 2007.

Edwards, Earl L., Lt. Col. Asst. Dir., Prisoner of War Division, Letter to Army Services Forces, regarding prisoner segregation, dated March 3, 1944, NARA RG 389, Entry 261, Box 2563. National Archives and Records Administration, College Park, MD

_____. Letter Regarding Prisoner Transfer, dated October 16, 1943, NARA RG 389, Entry 261, Box 2563. National Archives and Records Administration, College Park, MD

_____. Letter Regarding Prisoner Transfer, dated January 7, 1943, NARA RG 389, Entry 261, Box 2563. National Archives and Records Administration, College Park, MD

Enemy Prisoner of War Information Bureau. "World War II Enemy Prisoners of War Deceased in Theaters of Operations, Fort Holabird, MD, 2 July 1952", NARA RG 389, Entry 466, Box 1. National Archives and Records Administration, College Park, MD

Eppinga, Jane. *Death at Papago Park POW Camp: A Tragic Murder and America's Last Mass Execution*. Charleston, SC: The History Press, 2017.

Erichsen, Heino R. *The Reluctant Warrior: Former German POW Finds Peace in Texas*. Austin, TX: Eakin Press, 2001.

_____. Interview by author. October 7, 2002.

Fairchild, Byron and Jonathan Grossman. *United States Army in World War II: The War Department: The Army and Industrial Manpower*. Center of Military History, Department of the Army, Washington, DC, 2002.

Farrand, Stephen M. Major, Prisoner of War Operations Division, Letter to Special War Problems Division regarding the death of Karl Schaeffer, dated May 28, 1945, NARA RG 389, Entry 261, Box 2562. National Archives and Records Administration, College Park, MD

_____. Letter to Special War Problems Division regarding the death of Alfred Malinowski, dated February 20, 1945, NARA RG 389, Entry 261, Box 2562. National Archives and Records Administration, College Park, MD

"Find a Grave," Find a Grave, findagrave.com/.

Fischer, H. P., Office of the Commanding General, 9th Service Command, Fort Douglas, UT, Letter to Army Service Forces regarding new base camps, dated March 31, 1945, NARA RG 389, Entry 457, Box 1119. National Archives and Records Administration, College Park, MDFord, George. German Guard Held in Medical Ward After Shooting 28 Germans: Probe Opened by Army Into Salina Affair". The Deseret News, July 9, 1945.

Gansberg, Judith M., *Stalag: USA: The Remarkable Story of German POWs in America.* New York, NY: Thomas Y. Crowell Company, 1977.

German War Graves Commission at volksbund.de

Gimmeson, Johanna, *German POW Camp in Deaver, Wyoming, 1944–1945. 2001.*

Giordana, Beth. Interview by author. August 2001.

Griffith, L.E. Lt. Col., Prisoner of War Operations Division, Letter to Mrs. Ada Errera regarding transfer of body to Italy, dated April 30, 1946, NARA RG 389, Entry 261, Box 2562. National Archives and Records Administration, College Park, MD

Hamann, Jack. *On American Soil: How Justice Became a Casualty of World War II.* Algonquin Books, 2005.

Hanson, Tor. *Camp Abbot (Images of America).* Arcadia Publishing, 2018

Heisler, Barbara Schmitter. "Returning to America: German Prisoners of War and the American Experience", German Studies Review, Vol. 31, No. 3 (Oct. 2008), pp. 537–556; Published by The Johns Hopkins University Press on behalf of the German Studies Association

Heitmann, John A. "Enemies are Human." (Presentation, Dayton Christian-Jewish Dialogue, May 10, 1998).

Iannantuoni, Mario. Interview by author. February 10, 2012.

Jensen, Carol A. *Images of America: Byron Hot Springs.* San Francisco, CA: Arcadia Publishing, 2006.

Jones, L.B.C. Lt. Col. Deputy Director, Internal Security Division, Regarding Security, dated October 14, 1943, NARA RG 389, Entry 261, Box 2563. National Archives and Records Administration, College Park, MD

Keefer, Louis E., *Italian Prisoners of War in America, 1942–1946: Captives or Allies?* New York, NY: Praeger, 1992.

Kirkpatrick, Kathy. Italian POWs in Utah." (Presentation, TRACES conference, October 7, 2002)

_____ (Presentation, TRACES conference, May 31, 2003).

Kleinman, Steven M. "The History of MIS-Y: US Strategic Interrogation During World War II". Master's thesis, Joint Military Intelligence College, 2002.

Knappe, Siegfried & Ted Brusaw. *Soldat: Reflections of a German Soldier 1936–1949.* New York, NY: Orion Books, 1992.

Krammer, Arnold. "American Treatment of German Generals" The Journal of Military History 54, No. 1 (January 1990): 27–46.

_____. "German Prisoners of War in the United States" Military Affairs 40, No. 2 (April 1976): 68–73.

_____. *Nazi Prisoners of War in America.* Lanham, MD: Scarborough House, 1996.

Leighton, Richard M., and Robert W. Coakley. *The United States Army in World War II, The War Department, Global Logistics and Strategy 1940–1943*, Washington, DC: Office of the Chief of Military History, Department of the Army, 1955.

Lewis, George G, and John Mewha. *History of Prisoner of War Utilization by the United States Army, 1776–1945.* U.S. Department of the Army, Pamphlet 20-213, Washington, DC: Government Printing Office, 1955.

L'Ufficio Informazione Vaticano per I pregionieri di guerra istituito da Pio XII, Vatican Secret Archives. Vatican City.

Lucioli, Ezio. Interview by author. August 14, 2009.

Luick-Thrams, Michael. "The Fritz Ritz: German POWs in the American Heartland" (Presentation, TRACES conference, May 31, 2003).

Margotilli, Giuseppe. Interview by author. August 14, 2009.

Martin, Charles E., Col., Director of Personnel, Memorandum to Armed Service Forces, regarding release of ISU, dated October 3, 1945, NARA RG 389, Entry 261, Box 2563. National Archives and Records Administration, College Park, MD

_____. Memorandum to Armed Service Forces, regarding release of ISU, dated August 23, 1945, NARA RG 389, Entry 261, Box 2563. National Archives and Records Administration, College Park, MD

_____. Memorandum to Armed Service Forces, regarding release of ISU, dated August 20, 1945, NARA RG 389, Entry 261, Box 2563. National Archives and Records Administration, College Park, MD

Meier, Susan Ann, "Limited Freedom: The Italian Service Units in Southern California's Inland Empire During World War II". Thesis at California State University, Fullerton: 2004

Moore, John Hammond. Italian POWs in America: War is Not Always Hell." Prologue (Fall 1976): 141–151.

_____. *Wacko War: Strange Tales from America 1941–1945.* Raleigh, NC: Pentland Press, 2001.

Nagler, Joerg A. "Enemy Aliens and Internment in World War I: Alvo von Alvensleben in Fort Douglas, Utah, a Case Study." Utah Historical Quarterly 58 (Fall 1990): 388–406

Nash, Gerald D. *The American West Transformed: The Impact of the Second World War.* Bloomington, IN: Indiana University Press, 1985.

National Archives and Records Administration, Record Group 38. Records of the Navy; Special Activities Branch (OP-16-Z), Navy Unit, Tracy, California. National Archives and Records Administration, College Park, MD

_____. Record Group 331. Records of Allied Operational and Occupation Headquarters, World War II. Entry 3A, Box 126. Repatriation to USSR. National Archives and Records Administration, College Park, MD

_____. Record Group 389. Records of the Office of the Provost Marshal General. National Archives and Records Administration, College Park, MD

Orsini, August. Interview by author. October 7, 2011.

Palermo, Raffaele. "ISU Personnel Records." Al Ministero della Difesa, Rome, Italy.

Parri, Dino. *Il Giuramento; Generale a El Alamein, prigioniero in America (1942–1945).* Milano: Mursia, 2009.

"*Per il Soldato Francesco Erriquez la guerra è finita!*," *Un Mondo di Italiani*, unmondoditaliani.com/per-il-soldato-francesco-erriquez-la-guerra-e-finita.htm.

Pisani, Pat and Maria. Interview by author. June 12, 2009.

Powell, Allan Kent.*Splinters of a Nation; German Prisoners of War in Utah.* Salt Lake City, UT: University of Utah Press, 1989.

Prisoners in Paradise, DVD, directed by Camilla Calamandrei. 2001.

"Prisoners of War in Ogden: 1943–1946," Weber State University Stewart Library, library.weber.edu/asc/POW/default.cfm.

Pulia, Peter A., Sr. Interview by author. May 1, 2002.

Reiss, Matthias. "Bronzed Bodies behind Barbed Wire: Masculinity and the Treatment of German Prisoners of War in the United States during World War II." The Journal of Military History 69, No. 2 (April 2005): 475-504.

Richards, Su. Interview by author. May 23, 2009.

Rogers, John R. Interview by author. September 3, 2007.

Salgado, Rebecca C. "Rebuilding the Network: Interpretation of World War II Prisoner-of-War Camps in the United States." Master's Thesis, Columbia University, May 2012.

Scott, Ralph. "Violations of International Law in the Treatment of German POWs Following the Cessation of Hostilities". (Presentation, TRACES conference, June 1, 2003).

Selmi, Andrea. Interview by author. November 2, 2018.

Smith, Clarence McKittrick. *United States Army in World War II: The Technical Services: The Medical Department: Hospitalization and Evacuation, Zone of Interior.* Center of Military History, United States Army, Washington, DC, 2003.

Spidle, Jake W. Jr. "Axis Prisoners of War in the United States, 1942-1946: A Bibliographical Essay." Military Affairs 39, No. 2 (April 1975): 61–66.

"State Department-Related Sites: Hotels and Resorts," German American Internee Coalition, gaic.info/ShowPage.php?section=Internment_Camps_

Storm, Ralph A., *Camp Florence Days.* N.p. 2007.

Thomas, Jennie M. "History of the Prisoner of War Camp Utah ASF Depot, Ogden, UT", February 1, 1945.

Thompson, Antonio S., *Men in German Uniform: POWs in America during World War II*, Knoxville, TN: University of Tennessee Press, 2010.

Tissing, Robert Warren Jr. "Utilization of Prisoners of War in the United States During World War II: Texas, A Case Study". Master's Thesis, Baylor University, 1973.

Todaro, Robert J. Interview by author. June 12, 2006.

Togni, Fernando. Interview by author. August 14, 2009.

Tollefson, A.M., Col., Director, Prisoner of War Operations, Letter to Special Projects Division regarding the death of Giovanni Cincotta, dated January 10, 1946, NARA RG 389, Entry 462, Box 2562. National Archives and Records Administration, College Park, MD

_____. Letter to Special Projects Division regarding the death of Giovanni E. Bondini, dated June 8, 1945, NARA RG 389, Entry 261, Box 2562. National Archives and Records Administration, College Park, MD

_____. Letter to Special Projects Division regarding Salina shooting, dated August 28, 1945, NARA RG 389, Entry 261, Box 2562. National Archives and Records Administration, College Park, MD

Trezzani, Claudio. Letter from Monticello PW Camp, AR, dated January 26, 1944. Stato Maggiore Esercito, #2256A, Rome, Italy

Turrini, Marcello. Interview by author. November 22, 2016.

Ulio, J.A., Major General, the Adjutant General's office, letter to The Commanding Generals, dated April 9, 1943. NARA RG 389, Entry 261, Box 2563. National Archives and Records Administration, College Park, MD

University of Utah. *Historic Fort Douglas at the University of Utah, a Brief History & Walking Tour,* Salt Lake City, UT: University of Utah, 2000.

Urwiller, Clifford S., Col. Prisoner of War Operations Division, Memorandum for Camp Operations Branch regarding surplus ISU units, dated October 18, 1945, NARA RG 389, Entry 261, Box 2563. National Archives and Records Administration, College Park, MD_____. Memorandum for Camp Operations Branch regarding surplus ISU units, dated September 14, 1945, NARA RG 389, Entry 261, Box 2563. National Archives and Records Administration, College Park, MD

U.S. House. Report of Committee on Military Affairs. 78th Congress., 2nd sess., H. Res. 30.

U.S. House. Report of Committee on Military Affairs. 79th Congress., 1st sess., H. Res. 20.

Vecchio, Giovanni and Orazio. Interview by author. November 17, 2018.

War Department, to Commanding Generals, Regarding movement orders, dated November 14, 1945, NARA RG 389, Entry 261, Box 2563. National Archives and Records Administration, College Park, MD

_____. Regarding movement orders, dated November 1, 1945, NARA RG 389, Entry 261, Box 2563. National Archives and Records Administration, College Park, MD

_____. Regarding movement orders, dated October 23, 1945, NARA RG 389, Entry 261, Box 2563. National Archives and Records Administration, College Park, MD

_____. Regarding movement orders, dated September 18, 1945, NARA RG 389, Entry 261, Box 2563. National Archives and Records Administration, College Park, MD

Wardlow, Chester. *United States Army in World War II: The Technical Services: The Transportation Corps: Movements, Training, and Supply*. Center of Military History, United States Army, Washington, DC, 2003.

Weyand, A.M., Col. Commanding, Prisoner of War Camp, Ogden, UT, Letter regarding prisoner segregation, dated January 21, 1944, NARA RG 389, Entry 261, Box 2563. National Archives and Records Administration, College Park, MDWhittingham, Richard. *Martial Justice: the Last Mass Execution in the United States*. Bluejacket Books, Naval Institute Press, Annapolis, MD. 1997

Wilcox, Walter W. "The Wartime Use of Manpower on Farms." Journal of Farm Economics 28, No. 3 (Aug. 1946): 723–741.

Winter, Richard. "Hot Springs, NC. A World War I Internment Camp." *North Carolina Postal Historian* 27, no. 1 (2008)

"WWI German Prisoners of War in Utah," GenTracer, gentracer.org/WWIGermanPrisonersofWarinUtah.html.

"WWI Internment Camp in Hot Springs, NC: The German Village," Welcome to Madison County, North Carolina, visitmadisoncounty.com/who-we-are/town-of-hot-springs/the-german-village-wwi-internment-camp/.

Acknowledgments

Christine Saffell (researcher and travel companion)
Kate and John Saffell (website, data entry, photos)
Alessandro de Gaetano (producer, screenwriter of Red Gold)
Andrea Boni and family (son of Guido Boni, an Italian POW)
Andrea Selmi and family (son of Carlo Selmi, an Italian POW)
Barbara Harvey (Mother, support, great memory for events in her lifetime)
Betty Alberts, local historian in Douglas, WY
Carmelina Impellizzeri (daughter of Vincenzo Lo Giudice, an Italian POW)
Carol A. Jensen (historian and author)
Dave Kendziura (historian, Hill AFB)
Gina McNeeley (photographic expert, NARA researcher)
Jinger La Guardia (colleague who shares the goal of saving these "lost" stories)
Johanna Thompson, site director of Dubois Museum, WY
Karen Jensen and Pam Frisbie (my sisters who share the lure of the stories behind the headstones)
Karrie and Jenefer Jackson (data entry)
Kenneth D. Schlessinger (NARA II, College Park, MD)
Kent Powell (Utah Historical Society)
Marcello Turrini (son of Mario Turrini, an Italian POW)
Col. Maurizio Parri (grandson of General Dino Parri, an Italian POW)
Mel Glover, superintendent over Camp Douglas Museum
Michael Luick-Thrams (TRACES founder)
Michael Pomeroy (authority on Camp Monticello, AR)
Orazio and Giovanni Vecchio (son/nephew and grandson of Orazio and Angelo Vecchio, Italian POW brothers)
Rhonda Jackson and Lucia Rogers (researchers)
Sarah Langsdon (Special Collections, Weber State University)
Stefano Palermo (son of Raffaele Palermo an Italian POW)
Steven Banks, historian in Dubois, WY

Please contact the author at gentracer@gmail.com to share your knowledge about the prisoners of war stories, photos, letters, and artifacts that may be part of your family and local history.

Index